Acknowledgements

CW00408074

Mrs D, I was blessed to spend two years with before old age too
God. Mrs D passed away on the 8th September 2020, a day befor
Birthday. A whopping 126 years old in dog years. I miss her every
when my time is up.

A big shout out to my best friend Gordie the Jack Russel, who I have grown up with and who still
believes he can hide his treats from me! Him, my Nan and Gramps are very dear to my heart. Love
you all so much.

Gracie, my Border Collie sweetheart. I will always be in debt to you for all your unconditional love
and kindness. I miss you every day.

I would also like to thank my Mother, Bikkie for being the wonderful Mother she was. Even though
she existed in the worst possible conditions, she cherished her litter of pups and instilled her wisdom
and what she had learned about humans and life before being stolen. She would be so proud of me.

Also Barney my cat friend (RIP) Thank you for all your support, wisdom and Friendship.

Next, my human Mom and Dad. You guys are the best! Thank you for loving me and for giving me
such a happy and wonderful life. I love you all the dog bones in the world.
A big thank you to my Mom's God and to Anubis the dog God, for all their love and protection. They
sure looked after Mom and I and still do.

Lastly, to you who is reading my story, I hope you enjoy it. I have done my best to correct my
mistakes. If I missed a few I am really sorry. Thank you for supporting me and God Bess You.

With love and gratitude
Finley

Chapter 1

When you young, you have no idea where your life's path will take you. Little did I know all the twists and turns that lay ahead for me. Let me tell you my story.

We had started out a litter of ten puppies. Sadly I lost two sisters in the first few days of them being born. Mother's name was Bikkie. She would smile while recalling how the name came from her love of chocolate dunking biscuits. Now that I am all grown up, I can see where I get my sweet tooth from. Mother did the best she could under the circumstances. She made sure we all had enough milk. I never met my Dad.

She told us it was a strange dog she had never met before who was put in the cage with her for several days to make sure she would fall pregnant. She would go on to explain that it was a tough life being what she called a 'breeding bitch'

Once we were old enough to understand, she explained that the day would come when we would be taken away from her. With eight crying pups, she tried to explain that there was nothing she could do. When that day came, we had to all be strong and very brave.

She didn't know what the future held for us, but she prayed it was with a loving family that did not cage or hurt us. Mother had been caged since she was stolen while out on a walk with her loving family.

We loved listening to her stories about the days when she ran free and lived in a warm and loving home. Mother told us those stories often. Especially towards the end of our time together. Every story had such a calming effect on us pups.

Mother would go into detail about the various smells along the pavements. She called it 'doggy news' and would tell us 'You can pick up a lot about the dogs in the neighbourhood from sniffing their urine. You can tell if they are sick, healthy, what diet they on, and even if they happy.'

We also learnt from Mother that eating grass if you not feeling well, is the best medicine. It was something she had longed for while being caged. She would tell us 'if your stomach is upset, you constipated, or you just lacking in a bit of nutrition or fibre, always remember to eat some fresh green grass. You will feel better very quickly'

Poor Mother had lost her trust in humans and had long given up hope of ever being found. She had suffered a lot over the past few years. Her only comfort these days was fading memories of a time long ago where she had known kindness, warmth and protection. This was her dream for us, her puppies.

I remember it was very cramped, dirty and difficult in the cage with Mother and all us pups. We had so little space. Nowhere to play. We didn't even know what it was like to walk on the grass mother had described. Feel the softness under our paws or lie chewing on sticks that we had heard about. Instead our days were filled with the cries from the other puppies and their Mothers trying to console them.

Mother used to often tell us to be quiet because Aunty Rosey, a Labrador a few cages down from us was very ill. Aunty Rosey could no longer feed her puppies and as such, a few had been discovered dead in the cage. This upset the breeders because it meant they didn't make the money they had anticipated.

I remember there was Rosey the Labrador, Poppy the Pomeranian, Lola the Bulldog, Millie the Scotch Collie, Daisy the Siberian Husky and of course our Mother Bikkie the Australian Shepherd. All the breeders said Bikkie was beautiful, and a great steal.

All the mothers were extremely proud of their beautiful litter of puppies and each one would tell the other, certain attributes their children had. Aunty Millie the Scotch Collie, had a puppy who had what she described as a 'Blue Star' in his one eye and she was sure that was a lucky sign and that her little boy, would go onto have a wonderful life.

I remember giving Mother a hard time because I wanted to know why I had not got blue eyes when my brothers and sisters mostly had blue eyes and Aunty Millie's puppy had a star in his and I had nothing. She would laugh and tell me 'you have the most beautiful amber eyes of any I have seen. You have wolf eyes that are filled with expression and wisdom. Do you know how lucky it is to have such rich amber eyes? It means you will find the perfect home and be happy and loved all your life.' I liked that. I had expression and wisdom. So I didn't have a blue star, I had wolf eyes! It was good enough for me.

We would lie with Mother listening to all the chatter and shared stories. The common thread with all these Mothers was sadly they had all once upon a time, been living happily in a loving family and had either been stolen from their own garden or while out on a walk.

The Mothers would enthrall all of us pups with stories about walks in the woodlands, lying by open fires in a lounge, sleeping with humans on beds, playing with balls and Frisbees, being hugged, brushed and well fed. Holidays they had spent with their human family and some had even swum in things called lakes and oceans.

A life they would never see again. They all new that they would die in the cage they were in. Never would they feel or experience that safety and love from a human again. The only reason they were still alive, was because they could produce another litter for the ever demanding market.

It was a known fact that once a Mother could no longer produce, she was put to sleep if they had an ounce of compassion. More likely shot in the back yard or beaten with a club on the head. We had all witnessed the clubbing style of execution and it was very traumatic for everyone to see and hear the yelping that went deep into your soul. The blood spattered all over the floor and splashes against the wall.

I asked Mother once, why she had never tried to escape. I remember her answer 'Son, it is impossible. Many have tried to dig their way out over the years. All have failed and met with death or life changing injuries. Those of us who have been here for a while, know that it is futile.'

We as young puppies were terrified of the breeders. Mother would encourage us to go up to them when the cage was opened and be nice and maybe they would take pity and give us a nice home. Those of us brave enough, would try but we just got shouted at and shoved aside. Often spilling the only bit of water, we had to drink.

All the puppies, including Rosey's, Millie's, Daisy's, Poppy's and of cause Aunty Lola's knew that the day would come when we would be taken away from our Mothers. What no one knew was when that would be. All we could do was wait.

As we grew, we all became very anxious. The cage grew smaller and with now so little space to wee and poo, it really was stinky and very unpleasant. There was nothing Mother could do. We piled up with her in the one corner of the cage that was clean so we could all stay dry.

Mother was growing restless. Looking back, I think she knew the time was near. She was never harsh with us pups, but she was snappy and very irritable. Every time our cage was approached, we would all start crying and climb all over each other for protection. Turned out we had panicked for nothing. The water and food bowl would be filled up and the breeder would simply walk away. Leaving us to all calm down again.

The dreaded day came.

Us kids, had all been playing, biting each other and generally making a noise in our cage when Mother told us to be quiet, she needed to listen to the conversation between Breeder and Driver. 'Bring the trailer tomorrow at ten and we'll load them up along with the others' we heard the woman say.

'What does that mean mother?' we all asked in unison. 'My Darling Puppies. Come and sit down. The time has come. You must listen carefully to me. Our time together is limited. Tomorrow, you and your brothers and sisters, along with the other mother's puppies, will be taken away and sold to new homes. Many of you will travel on long journey's'

She went on to say 'You must stay strong. Never lose your dream of finding that forever home. You are all going to need to be very brave. Take care of each other as best you can until you are separated. Remember not all humans are cruel. Remember your Mother once had a loving and wonderful home. Never lose hope of finding that happy home with a family that loves you.

Learn from my mistake. Never stray too far from your owners. Don't be tempted to wonder off on your own or where you cannot be seen by your owner. If you are blessed to go to a good home, be loyal to your owner, protect them, and bring them love, healing and comfort. Be strong my puppies. You are Australian Shepherds, and as such, you are not only beautiful, but intelligent, loyal and protective. All fine qualities each of you has. All will be fine.'

It was a long, sad, miserable night. We, including Mother were crying and desperately trying to comfort each other. Mother at one point was howling like a wolf along with Aunty Daisy the Siberian Husky. That last night, she cleaned each and every one of us. She licked and licked until we were all clean and comforted. I remember she never ate that night, so we could all have food in our bellies. She wasn't sure when or where our next meal would come from.

With her broken spirit she was still trying to reassure us as we one by one got picked up and tossed into a cage on the back of a trailer.

Just before I got put into the cage, I remember turning around and taking one last look at my beautiful Mother. She had her snout pushed as far through the iron bars as it would go. Her intense stare was haunting. She had a dignified, yet desperate look in her blue eyes. I could see the pain, tears and desolation as she watched us one by one disappear into the cage. I sometimes still see her face in my dreams today.

Once Aunty Rosey's surviving puppies were loaded, along with Aunty Lola's, Aunty Daisy's, Aunty Poppy's and Aunty Millie's, a dark cover was thrown over all the cages and all light disappeared. With our vision taken, our hearing was acute. The truck pulled off. The crying from the Mothers and their caged puppies on the truck filled the air. I thought I would die from the pain in my chest. I was so scared.

As we drove away from the farm. I buried my head in my paws and whimpered. I knew I would never see our dear Mother again. What would become of her? Where were these people taking us? I tried so hard to remember everything my Mother had tried to teach us and the stories of happier times running free.

I was the first-born puppy and therefore it was my duty to be strong for my brothers and sisters. The road was very bumpy, and we kept banging into each other.

You couldn't hear yourself think for all the crying. Thirty two terrified puppies can be quite deafening. Over the crying and hysteria, I tried telling Mothers stories of running free through woodlands. Chasing squirrels up trees and Fetching tennis balls.

Swimming in lakes. Lying chewing on bones. Lying on the sofa with your head on a cushion. But most of all, I tried to remind all the puppies that not all humans are bad. Our Mother was sure we would all find a loving home.

My small stories seemed to bring little comfort. I was so tired and we were all hungry. We were on that trailer for a long time before it came to a stop. I heard people talking outside the truck.

'I have Pomeranians, Bulldogs, Labradors, Siberian Huskies, Scotch Collies, and Australian Shepherds. How many of each do you want?' The deal was agreed, something called money was paid and suddenly we were in the light again. The dark canvas had been lifted and we were all being inspected.

'These puppies are sick!' The man said after looking at Aunty Rosey's puppies. 'No they well. They just car sick. Nothing wrong with them. I don't sell you sick puppies. You know I am good for breeding' said the man that used to sometimes feed us back in the cage. The man was lying. We all knew Aunty Rosey's Labrador puppies were sick.

'If these puppies die, I expect a full refund. I only want bitches. I will take this one, that one, and the black one at the back.' Said the man. The man continued going through the cages picking the breed and sex of the puppies he wanted.

I lost my sisters on that stop. Although I was tired, my paws were sore from being in the cage for so long and I was feeling very weak, I was so happy that he had not picked me. I didn't like him at all. He was rough, unkind and I picked up a smell that was familiar to me from the dark, dank bunker we were born in. He was one of the, 'not so nice humans'

Once business was concluded the canvas was pulled back over the cages and the truck began moving. Not long after that we stopped again. More puppies got picked and money was exchanged. Again, I didn't get picked. That night we stayed in the cage. I heard the driver saying to someone on the phone 'tomorrow we cross the border into the UK'

Where on Earth the UK was, I didn't know but the driver had said it was going to be a long drive and they had to be very careful they were not caught at the border and to use the connections they had where possible. We were only a few puppies now. Of the Australian Shepherds, it was only my brother and I left. I remember catching a glimpse of who I think was 'Blue Star' in one of the other cages. I saw a bluish tint in his one eye, and was surprised he had not been taken.

From listening to the conversation, we had been pre-selected. That explained why we had not been chosen with the previous two stops. We were going to a place called Reading in the UK as there were two buyers waiting for our arrival.

We had not eaten since the previous night and not had any water either. The driver and his companion did not want to feed us because he didn't want to risk us being sick. He also didn't want to have to clean up before dropping us at our destination. It was a long uncomfortable and thirsty night.

As the sun rose in the morning, the driver climbed into the truck and we were off again. Next stop the UK. Would he make it through this thing called a border? Many hours later we arrived at what I can only assume was the border. There the driver was asked many questions and gave answers I never understood. To be honest, we were all too exhausted and weak to make a sound.

In fact, it wasn't long after that border place, the van stopped the canvas was pulled up and then pulled down once he had seen we were still alive. His money was still secure.

Finally, after three days on the road and being in that cage, the truck came to its final stop. This was it. We had arrived in the place called Reading. The canvas was lifted, and we were picked up, inspected, and put into our various cages or in my brother and my case, a wooden outdoor hut. We had been separated from the other puppies. Unbeknown to me at the time, it would be six years until my path would cross with 'Blue Star' again.

It was a woman who had bought us, and she would be selling us on. As far as people go, she didn't seem too bad. I didn't get such a bad smell or sense anything to be fearful of. That night we got given some porridge and water for the first time in days. My brother and I were very weak.

We only managed a mouth full and we were asleep on a mound of hay. I must say, after growing up in a cage, and being on that truck in a cage for over three days, the hay was a welcome relief. My paws were so sore, and my body ached from standing on the steel bars. I didn't know who I had been reserved for or where either of us would end up.

I just remember the day my life changed forever. It was a really hot day in June 2014. We had been in this hut and on the hay for days. Between my brother and I, we kept knocking our water over which didn't help because the woman only checked on us once a day.

Because of the intense heat, we were so thirsty. There was not a drop of water to share. Nothing. We were suffocating and growing weaker by the hour. It had all been too much on our young bodies. There were no windows and not a breath of air was coming into the wooden hut standing in the midday sun with not a leaf of shade.

I sensed my brother was dying. His fighting spirit was ebbing. Since we arrived I had heard the woman talk of him being sold for a lot of money as a stud.

'He has blue eyes and good colours in his coat. We can make money from this one' It was true, he had taken after Mother with his bright blue eyes. What a stud was, I didn't know then. Whatever that meant, looking at my brother, I didn't think he would ever live to see that life.

On what would turn out to be our last day together, I kept trying to wake him and play with him to keep his spirits up. It wasn't working. He had no energy. We were both sick. Since we had arrived in this place called Reading, we were vomiting and had really bad runny tummies both of which were meshed in with the hay we lay on.

That's when I heard her voice. I will never in my life forget that voice. It was a woman who had come to buy one of the puppies. I couldn't see her. All I could do was listen.

'Hello, I'm Danny and I have come to collect a Border collie puppy. We spoke on the phone' she said. I couldn't quite make out the rest of the conversation. What I heard next was the same kind voice I had heard earlier asking the woman 'What is in that wooden hut?' the woman answered her saying 'No you can't have one of those, they are reserved. Besides, they are not Border Collies. The puppies in there are Australian Shepherds. I will go and fetch you a Border collie puppy'

'No, I want to see the puppies in that wooden hut!' I heard her insist. Next minute the top of the stable door opened and fresh air entered into my almost collapsed lungs. I had to get out of here. I had to try and walk to the door. I desperately wanted her to notice me and take me out of this place.

I remember she bent over the door looked at my brother, looked at me and shook her head. She had tears in her eyes. She had a look similar in her eyes to that of my Mother the last time I saw her. I recognized the loneliness. The sadness. With my last bit of energy, I stumbled to her dangling hand. I nuzzled her hand and stood on my back legs and lent into her arm.

She picked me up and held me close. I was too weak to even give her a kiss by licking her hand or her face. 'I will take this puppy' she told the woman who was not happy because I had been reserved.

Danny was having none of it and went on with her voice calm but firm 'This puppy is weak and dying. Do you even know what the temperature is today? Its 34 degrees and there is not a drop of water in that hut. These puppies are sick and this boy needs a vet before he dies in my arms. Now you can either take my money, let me leave with this puppy or I can phone the RSPCA. The choice is yours. What will it be?'

Danny paid the woman, opened the car door and I was placed on the back seat where I subsequently weed. I tried to hold it in, but I couldn't. As we drove out the yard, the car stopped and my new Mother made a call to the place called the RSPCA and she reported the woman. She explained she had thought she was going to a legit breeder and it turned out to be a puppy farm. I had heard that before. I saw my mother's face flash before my amber eyes.

She then picked me up and said 'You are so beautiful, but you also stinky, full of wee and poo and you sick. I am taking you home to give you a bath, give you something to eat and drink then we off to the vet to fix you up. I will think of a name for you over the coming days, but you safe now. I will look after you always. That I promise you.'

With that, I was plonked back on the seat and off we drove. She left the back window open for me and it was the most amazing experience. The wind was blowing my ears back.

Chapter 2

My new Mother parked the car, picked me up and carried me into the house, up the stairs, and into the bathroom. I never saw much of anything. I was to have a bath to wash the wee and poo off my coat. Once she had run the bath water, I was ceremoniously plonked into the warm water and shampoo was rubbed into my coat.

I decided on that day, that this bathing malarkey was not for me! Other dogs may enjoy it, but I was not going to be one of them. She scrubbed and scrubbed, rinsed, and just before I could get my shaking off the water thing going, she wrapped me up in a thick heavy towel.

I couldn't wait for all this fuss to be over with. I had even forgotten how sick I felt with all the nonsense of putting me in a bath. I got carried downstairs and put down on the kitchen floor. I remember it felt so strange under my paws. My new Mother put down some food in a bowl for me and next to that a bowl of water, both of which I finished in record time.

'Time for the vet boy. Common' she called. I wasn't sure what I was meant to do until she called me with her hands and a strange sound she made with her mouth. Like a kissing sound. 'Common muah muah' as I started walking towards her, she would say 'good boy. Common, let's go' and more of those kissy sounds. I got it in the end and understood what I was meant to do.

I followed her back to the car.

'What is your puppy's name?' the vet asked. 'I haven't named him yet. I only picked him up about two hours ago from a puppy farm. The conditions that this poor animal was living in were shocking. I need you to please check him over' she said.

I don't know what happened. I was trying to be quiet and goodly, but the next minute I was vomiting and pooing at the same time. Urgh there were these things coming out of my mouth and bum. 'What the hell is that?' I heard my Mother ask.

'It's live worms. Poor puppy is not in the best condition. He is malnourished, underweight and quite clearly full of worms. Probably never been dewormed. Don't worry little fellow, we will fix you up in no time at all' The vet said while stroking me.

I liked this man. I could smell he was kind and I didn't even mind when he gave me an injection. I sat quietly and afterwards my Mother said she was very proud of me because I was so well behaved and such a good boy.

Actually I remember feeling a whole lot better after vomiting up those live worms. Or maybe it was the injection? No it was the food and water. Oh I can't be sure, but I did feel a whole lot more like a puppy should after a few hours of being with my new Mother.

The best part of my first day in my new home was when we got back from the vet. I was allowed to run on the grass, and I met my new best friend. My Mothers Niece called Willow. She was four years old and she gave me lots of hugs and kisses and we chased each other around the trees for what seemed like ages. I liked her very much. Willow lived a few doors down from my Mother so she would become one of my best friends, along with Barney her cat.

Willow is all grown up now and she is still one of my favourite people. I will always remember the love and kindness I felt when I was playing with her that first day of my new life.

It was an action packed first day for a puppy like me who had been to hell and back and who didn't think he would live to see the dawn of a new day. I did pine for my brother and I heard my Mother telling my Nan while watching Willow and I play on the grass, 'God Mom, my heart broke looking at these poor puppies. The conditions they were living in was disgusting. I had no choice. I could only take one puppy. I just wish I had more money. I would have taken both the puppies. This boy's brother was dying. Maybe I could have saved him if I had the money to buy him. I just hope and pray that the RSPCA went there, and those poor animals were taken to safety. There were cages and cages of crying puppies. Heartbreaking.'

My mother has said on numerous occasions since then 'I should have just taken them both and walked out telling that bloody woman, to phone the police!'

Those first few days were a whirlwind. My Mothers partner Ryan came home that first night and was not happy to see me on the sofa. He and my Mother had an argument and he tried very hard that first evening to persuade her to get rid of me. He kept telling her 'What the hell are you going to do with a bloody dog? We have two cats is that not enough for you? How are you ever going to look after a dog? You going to end up having to get rid of it. If that bloody dog upsets my cats there will be hell to play' and on and on it went.

I felt so sorry for my Mom. Over the next few days I would see her crying a lot from some of the nasty things Ryan would say to her. She would phone my Nan and talk for hours about her relationship. Most of it to be honest I was too young to understand and these were human emotions I had not learned yet.

When he wasn't there, we would have such fun. My mother introduced me to the cats, who hated my guts. I was fascinated by those fur balls and all I wanted was to put my nose into their fur coats and play with them. They were having none of it. They were snobby and would talk about how stupid I was, how clumsy and how their lives had changed for the worse since I had arrived.

When Ryan wasn't there, they would tolerate me. When Ryan arrived home, they would play up to him and make out that I was this bad puppy who they were terrified of and that their lives were so unbearable. That of course would spark another fight between my Mom and Ryan. It seemed that every day there was an argument and Ryan would bully my Mom. I began to really dislike those cats because I knew what they were up to and my poor Mother was non the wiser. I also began to distance myself from Ryan. He made my Mother cry too much and I didn't like that one bit.

I did have one cat friend in the first few months and that as I mentioned, was Barney. He would come and visit me every day and we would eat our dinner together and he would allow me to nuzzle him. He was a cool cat and he liked the nibbles my Mother always gave him. So I guess not all cats are bad.

Besides, Barney was 'too fat to run away from Finley's nuzzles' my Mother would tell my Nan. They would laugh and say Barney was a striped Garfield. I had no idea who Garfield was but he must have been fat because Barney was fat that's for sure, but he was my only animal friend and I liked him. Come to think of it, now that I am grown up, I have met a few 'Garfields' so it must mean fat cat.

After a few days I had a name! Man was that hard work! Everyone was saying 'Call him this. Or call him that. What about Charlie, Max, blah blah' My Mother had already come up with the name Finley, which I rather liked but everyone was trying to name me. So she decided she would pick four names and for four days she would call me a new name each day to see which one she preferred and I liked.

That was a dodgy time. The only name I liked was Finley and I was beginning to think she was never going to call me that so when the fourth day came and it was 'Finley' day, I really made sure she understood that I was a 'Finley' and not Charlie, Max or Walter! I mean what was she thinking? Walter? So Finley it was.

Life was very upside down those first few weeks. Everything my Mother did was wrong in Ryan's eyes. She was spoiling me too much. She didn't discipline me enough. I was taking advantage of her. She needed to be the pack leader, the alpha dog. Whatever that meant. He would call me 'that bloody dog' He even decided one day to put a child gate on the staircase so his cats could be safe from me.

He would moan at my Mother if she forgot to close and lock the gate. His cats were everything and I was the worst mistake my Mother had made according to him. A waste of bloody money he would say.

Then one day my heart got broken. I heard my Mother sobbing on the phone to her friend Jessica. In the short time I had been with my new mom, I had heard Jessica's name a lot and listened to many conversations on loud speaker. She used to be my Mom's boss and they became the best of friends. My Mom always said how grateful she was to have Jessica in her life.

'Jessica it's just causing so much trouble. I love Finley with all my heart, but I can't take the insults and arguing any more. I'm beginning to think Ryan is right. Maybe buying Finley was wrong and I won't be able to look after him. What if I lose my home? Or I lose my job? Please ask the farmers in your area if they want to give Finley a good home. Please Jessica it must be the best home ever. I am heartbroken, but what can I do? Ryan is making our lives so miserable and it's affecting Finley too and it's not fair. He is an innocent puppy and deserves better than this'

That day, I remember thinking, well yes, it is affecting me, but please don't give me away. I love you so much and I don't want to be with anyone else. I will love you and protect you and will always be there for you, please, please don't give me away. Ryan doesn't affect me, it's your crying and loneliness that does.

I just wished I could tell her how sorry I was for chasing the cats and how I will never do it again if she just lets me stay.

Eating dinner with Barney that night, I told him about the conversation I had overheard. Barney told me a story of a time when his Mom and Dad had to put him into kennels because their circumstances had changed. They loved Barney and the only way to keep him safe was to put him temporally into kennels until their circumstances changed. He told me not to lose hope.

I remember him saying to me 'A man like Ryan who thinks he is wise, must be avoided. Your Mother will come to her senses Fin, you'll see.'

That was very difficult to believe at the time. I was only three months old. Today I look back with wisdom but at the time it was so difficult to understand. I could hear all the arrangements taking place. New owners had been found and the following day I was going on a two hour drive and was to be handed over to a couple who had a big yard and who were very excited to have me moving in.

That last night with my Mother was awful. For the second time in my short life, I was losing a mother. I wouldn't leave her side. She sat with me on her lap, a bottle of wine on the table and a toilet roll to mop up her tears. She kept telling me how much she loved me and how sorry she was that it had come to this. She was begging my forgiveness. I could do nothing but give her all the love I had left in me.

That following morning we were meant to be on the road early and I couldn't lift my tail at all. I was so very sad and so scared to leave my new mom whom in a short space of time I had grown to love so much.

Barney came over in the morning to see how I was and I told him we 'hitting the road early' because that is what I had heard my Mother saying to Jessica last night. I told him I had tried everything to change my Mothers mind but it hadn't worked. He purred and rubbed himself up against me. Giving me as much comfort as he could.

'Hang in there kid. I can sense something in the air. I'm never wrong. I'm a cat, my sixth sense is always spot on. Pick your tail up boy nobody likes a dog with a tail between his legs'

Then everything just happened all at once. My Mother and I were downstairs with Barney when Ryan came out his bedroom. He had been sleeping in the spare room for ages because of me. He wanted to sleep with his cats and my Mom wanted to sleep with me. So all a bit awkward really.

'So what time are you getting that dog out of here so my cats can go back to a normal life?' he asked.

'I'm not. I have cancelled everything. I have decided that Finley is staying and you and the cats are leaving. I have had enough Ryan. It's over. It's all over!' she replied.

'What's that supposed to mean?' he shouted back at her

'Ryan, you have made mine and Finley's life utterly miserable for too long now. To the point where I have found this poor puppy another home and why? All because you are a selfish bastard who cares only about himself. I have decided that if anyone is leaving this house, it is you! So please make the necessary arrangements to move out. In the meantime, you will leave Finley alone, and I will try and keep him away from your cats as best I can' she replied.

Oh man was Ryan furious. The fight was on again. I was in shock and Barney called me into the kitchen and said 'stay out the way boy. Here, I have left you a few treats, let your Mother finish this. I told you, I am never wrong!' So I stayed in the kitchen with Barney until the drama was over.

The insults were flying and my Mother was standing her ground. She accused him of taking fourteen years of her life and how stupid she had been to allow him to do so. She told him he was a narcissist prick and shouted 'close the bloody door on your way out, and you leave Finley alone. No more picking on him or giving him or myself a hard time. It's over! Take your cats and move out.'

'You choosing a fucking dog over me?' he shouted.

'No Ryan. I am choosing life over you. I have been ridiculed, and made to feel worthless and not good enough for far too long. I have forgotten who I am. The lines between right and wrong have been smudged. My blind love or more likely co-dependency has allowed you to get away with far more than you deserve. You have complexed me beyond belief and I no longer know who I am. I have forgotten what it's like to laugh and be happy. I have convinced myself that this is what a relationship is all about. If I just try a little harder. Or if I can just change this, or that about me and so it goes on.

You are a bully and it excites you to see me so miserable. You play with my emotions. You've just taken it up a notch since Finley arrived six weeks ago. If you not gunning for me, you gunning for Finley. So no, I am not choosing a fucking dog over you, I am choosing life and happiness over you. Finley brings me happiness and joy deep into my being.' I heard her say

'Did you hear that Fin? Everything will be just fine. Learn the word 'Faith' Finley. It will lighten your path and destiny.' Purred Barney who was well chuffed that he had foretold this event.

'What is faith?' I asked Barney.

'Well Finley, faith is having confidence or trust. It's just knowing and believing in your heart that bad things will become good' answered Barney. I made a mental note of that. Wise old fat cat.

It took ages for things to calm down and Barney left me alone after a while because my mom's sister was calling him. He told me he had spent the night at the neighbour's because they feed him tuna. So he hadn't been home in two days and best he go. He told me to stay where I was until I was called otherwise I will just get in the way. So I did exactly that, I stayed in the kitchen until I heard my Mom.

'Common Finny, let's go to the lake for a walk and you can have a swim.' I felt uneasy walking through the lounge past Ryan. On the walk, my Mother phoned Jessica and explained everything and I knew I was safe. I didn't know how life would change, but I knew it would never be the same again. At the lake she sat down on the bench, took my face in her hands and said 'I am sorry Finley' she said a whole lot more but I couldn't hear her. She had covered my ears with her hands and was kissing my snout, later to be affectionately called my 'hooter' but I understood we were a team and all the drama of me leaving was over. I was here to stay and we were going to grow old together.

We walked around the lake, I got into trouble for chasing the ducks and almost got nipped by a giant swan who was in no mood for my antics. We were at the lake for ages. I don't think my Mom wanted to go home and face Ryan again. Neither did I to be honest. It was peaceful and fun at the lake. Loads of dogs, puppies, squirrels and kids. Eventually we made our way back to the house.

The fighting was over. Ryan told my Mom that he was moving out and that he would be gone in the next couple of months and that she was to keep me away from his cats and not to allow me to traumatize them when he wasn't there. As if, I did that!

After that day of shouting, everything just calmed down. Ryan even patted me every now and then. He ignored my Mom whenever she spoke to him, and although I was still very young, I could feel the underlying tension between them.

Then one day I was playing outside with a new ball Mom had bought me, I must have been around five months old and I jumped up to bite the ball and when I landed I broke my leg. Ryan had just arrived home from work and was locking the car and he heard my leg bone snap. He rushed over and told my Mom to keep me still and calm and he would do a makeshift stretcher to put me on so I could be taken to the vet.

Ryan was very kind that day. He really did try very hard to make me comfortable and was really very concerned about my leg. I had gone into shock. I remember crying out once and then just shaking like a leaf. The pain was excruciating. My Mother was stressing and Ryan told her to pull it together.

I got lifted and placed on a piece of plank that Ryan had in his garage and he had covered it with a blanket to make it soft enough for me to lie on. Breaking my leg forced my Mom and Ryan to work as a team for those few minutes. It wasn't long and I was put onto the back seat of the car and driven to the Surgery.

Once I arrived I was taken off the 'stretcher' and placed in a cage. They told my Mother that the surgery was closed as it was Easter long weekend and that I would be operated on in three to four days' time. My Mom was so upset that I was going to be lying there with a broken leg for all those days. She kicked up a big fuss, but all the fussing was not going to change the public holiday long weekend. In the end, they told her she can come and visit me every day and assured her that me having to wait would not cause further damage to my leg. She was not happy but really had no choice but to accept it.

Mom came to visit me every single day. She would sit on the floor in front of the cage, open the door and stroke me. I was very drugged and couldn't really move much, but I would rest my head in her hands and she would tell me stories about her day.

She always brought me some tit bits, like little pieces of steak, or chicken. I remember I didn't eat much. I wasn't hungry at all. I was in a lot of discomfort and more than a little confused. Mom also brought me her slipper that I had chewed and use to carry around with me, and my favourite toy, a stuffed elephant that my Nan had given me. Come to think of it, I still have that elephant today and I am now six! Yes I was a bit of a chewer in my early days. Got into a lot of trouble for that, but it was such fun.

The four days to be honest, went by pretty quickly. I slept most of the time. On the Tuesday a lovely man came and took me out the cage. When I woke up, my leg had this great big steel contraption on it with pins going through my bone. I also had one of those umbrellas around my neck. I had seen dogs walking in the woods with those horrible things on and never understood why. Perhaps they had all broken their leg like I had. My leg felt double its weight from the steel bracket and with the umbrella, I was very unhappy.

The Doctor told my Mom she had to keep me caged for 23 hours a day and that I was not to run, or walk for more than 20 minutes a day on my leg. The collar had to stay on for a min of 6-8 weeks.

When I got home Ryan carried me into the house and put me in this horrible steel thing, I understood what the word 'cage' meant. I was not impressed. Looking back, I gave my

Mother the hardest time. I would cry and perform for hours on end. It was a big cage and I could stand up and turn around easily, and maybe even take a step or two, but it was a cage all the same and I didn't like it one bit.

I laugh when I look back or share my experiences with other dogs. My poor Mother really had a tough time. I would bark, cry, chew at the bars, and generally create as much noise as possible to get out of the cage. I used to get the steel frame on my leg caught between the bars and cry from the pain. I lost count how many trips we took to the vet.

My Mom had Ryan to deal with and Ryan, I came to understand had more than a slightly spiteful personality. The one morning he let me out my cage while my Mom was sleeping. It was early hours, maybe around 04h30 and Ryan was drinking tea and stroking his cats in the kitchen. He leant over and much to my surprise, opened the cage gate and let me hobble out.

Of course, I saw the cats and they were just taunting me 'Catch us if you can! Common doggie.' So I decided to chase them up the garden with my steel frame on. Ryan didn't stop me, he had the door to the garden open, a cup of tea in one hand and a smoke in the other. He watched me hobble up the distance of our small garden. Once I had reached the end, I heard him shouting up the stairs to my Mom 'Danny your dog has escaped and has chased my cats up the garden'

That was a lie, I had not escaped. He had let me out the cage and almost encouraged me to hobble after his cats. I was no threat to them in my state, and in fact I never had been. All I ever wanted was to play with them and make friends.

My mom came bounding down the stairs, half asleep and frantic because of the damage I would do to my leg. She accused Ryan of lying and said there was no way in hell I could have opened the cage door on my own. He must have opened it and let me out knowing full well, I would chase the cats and it was all out of spite.

Ryan told her she was a 'fucking mad bitch who needed counselling and how dare she accuse him of doing something like that' as I say, she was right. I had not opened the cage and everything she accused Ryan of was correct and she had no way of knowing.

I felt so sorry that I had lost control and 'chased' those fur balls. My Mom was very upset and Ryan just kept telling her how mad she was. I was put back in the cage and the fighting continued. I remember the cats had knocked some of the washing from the dining room table and Ryan had picked his stuff up and left my Mothers on the floor and he, the cats and myself had walked all over it. In fact he had his feet on my mother's clothing when she ran down the stairs.

Mom was really upset and asked him why he had not picked up hers when he collected his own from the floor. 'Why should I? It's your clothing not mine and if you didn't pay so much attention to the bloody dog, you would have taken it upstairs last night!'

My mind was now made up. The sooner this man left, the better. He was no good for my Mother and I would never put my Mom through this drama again. She deserved better than this and I realized that watching all the drama. He was a liar and he did play mind controlling games with her.

She checked that gate door a hundred times and she knew it was impossible for me to open, but Ryan was not about to change his lie. He had my Mother where he wanted her and that was stressed out, worried, tearful, and utterly miserable.

Well that little lie from Ryan resulted in me having to go back into theatre for another op on my leg. My whole steel frame had moved and my healing bone had been broken again.

Only this time, on hearing the story from my Mother, the vet asked her if it would be easier for her if he kept me for a few weeks at the surgery. I, by all accounts, needed 4 weeks of limited movement to allow the bone to heal. After that, she could pick me up and continue the treatment at home, but at least this way, I would be guaranteed of not disturbing the break again.

It made sense, and even though I was utterly miserable at the prospect of not being with my Mom, I understood that it was the best thing for all of us. It would ease the tension at home and allow my Mother to sort out her life without the worry of me 'escaping' again. So I didn't make a fuss and I behaved myself when she said goodbye and told me she would visit every day.

Look, I am not going to say I 'enjoyed' my time at the Surgery, but they were really nice to me. I liked all the staff and they checked on me all the time. They gave me treats, they chatted about my progress and used to say what a lovely woman my Mother was when she left.

So to be fair, it was not such a hardship and the time flew by. Four weeks went in the blink of an eye and on leaving, they gave me the most wonderful bed with the wording Snoozzee written all over it which I still have to this day. All those people fussed over me and even though my bone healed in the shape of a 'S' and today I have a limp, I will be forever grateful to them for saving my leg.

My mom still had another four weeks of nursing me, but I had turned the corner now which made life a little easier. On returning home, my Mom decided I was not going to be put back in the cage. Although the vet recommended it, it was not a necessity.

She would also in a few days find a way to allow me to take this umbrella off and not chew at the skin that had grown onto the steel rods going through my bone and into the frame.

So every morning without fail, she would dress my leg and wrap bandages over the steel frame. Making it impossible for me to chew through, and allowing me to recover by lying on my Snoozzee bed or the sofa without the umbrella.

Actually I became rather proficient at walking on three legs and not putting much strain on my broken leg.

The day I arrived home, I could see things in my absence had changed. Ryan had started packing and the house was full of boxes which made it a bit tricky walking around. Ryan and the cats were not happy to have me back and all three of them were still passing nasty remarks.

But like Barney would say 'What defines us kid, is how well we rise after falling' He was right. Mom and I were rising well together and determined to live our happiness. She would tell my Nan that every day she is finding another piece of her backbone.

Strange thing I noticed when I got back, was there was always this shadow walking with Ryan. A shadow of a man dressed in black and I didn't like the energy of that man. I would bark at it and my Mom thought I am barking at Ryan and would tell me to stop it.

The day Ryan finally moved out with his cats, we were standing in the garden to keep out the way while he carried boxes and loaded the van. My Mom said out loud and to nobody in particular 'What the hell is that following Ryan? It's a ghost, but not one with a good energy at all!'

So she did see it! Wow my Mother was more dog than I had realized! We stayed out in the garden until the front door closed and we saw Ryan and his ghost drive off. I saw a really strange side of my Mom that day. She walked around waving her hands in the air, drawing imaginary pictures into the air, spraying some kind of stuff into the air and every corner of the house.

I found out later while she was telling Jessica the story that she had done some cleansing, to get rid of Ryan's negativity and to bring peace and harmony back into our home. So that's what all that fuss was about. She was performing Reiki on our home. I would grow up seeing her doing this ritual a few times. Actually, if I am fair, I think it did actually work.

I often saw what I now know as ghosts, around my Mother, but they were always really nice people. She didn't see them, but I certainly did. She suspected they were there, because I would try and show her with barking at a particular spot, where they were standing. She would say to me, 'do we have company today Fin?' She is so smart my Mother.

We had a lot of cleaning up to do once Ryan had left. Mom changed the whole house around and rearranged the furniture. At one point, it looked like we were the ones moving out. But it all came together and she had done a great job, including dismantling that awful cage I had spent time in.

Four weeks went in the blink of an eye. I was back at the vet, back in theatre, and hurray, when I woke up this time, the metal contraption was off my leg. We could go home now and I could live a normal life again. My mother decided the sea water would be good for my closing wounds and good for her soul. So we jumped into her old camper van called Horrid Henry and off to the beach we went.

That was the most exciting thing of my life. I had never seen the sea before let alone swum in it. I remembered my real Mothers stories of her loving family taking her to the beach. How I wished she could see me now. How I wished, I could just see her one more time so she could see what a fine boy I was growing into and what a wonderful mother and family I had been lucky enough to go to. She was right all along, my wolf eyes were indeed a sign of great fortune and happiness.

I swam and swam, I chased, and ran with all the dogs, it was the best day ever. I forgot all about my past two months of pain and discomfort. It was the best two days of fun I had, had in ages.

Life from that moment just seemed to grow and develop into something calm and happy. I was losing my baby teeth, and my mom was picking them up and saving them.

We became, each other's lives. She would tell people that I had saved her life. When in truth, she had saved mine. I would do anything for her. I would protect her with my own life and I know she would do the same for me. We are one person. Again, I remembered my real Mothers advice 'never stray too far from your owner, be loyal and protect them' I never leave my Mom's side and she knows how deeply I love her and the deep gratitude I will always have for her saving my life and being the wonderful person she is to me.

Chapter 3

A dreaded call from our Landlady came through. From what I could gather she must have had a Ryan in her life too. She phoned my Mom crying and said she needed her cottage back because she had to move out.

Apparently her bloke had also been really mean to her and they had broken up. She had young twins from a thing called IVF treatment. I must say, watching humans, their lives are very strange. Everyone I have met so far, seems to have a Ryan in their life and so much misery and uncertainty.

I'm so glad I am a dog and not a human. These people are complicated beyond anything I can understand.

Whatever and however, the fact remained, we had to move. So my Mother and I began looking at houses on the internet. She would say to me 'What about this one Fin? This looks nice' and later find out that no dogs were allowed. Or 'Nope, that garden is smaller than the postage stamp you have right now. No good.' She had sixty days to find us a home that would allow me to live there.

This was proving difficult for her and she was forever walking around talking to herself and muttering 'Please God, let me find somewhere that I can take Finley' Well, whoever God is, he answered her by showing her a beautiful cottage on a working farm with a huge garden and the bonus was they had no problem with me moving in with her.

The first day she took me there to look, I was amazed. The garden was massive. I had more than enough yard to bury my bones and play football with my Mom. This was way cool. Only thing I didn't like, was there were a few too many men around there. Working of course, but still. I had become very protective of my Mother and after all I had seen so far, men were not to be trusted and I was going to keep every one of those away from my mother!

Moving day like most things, came around rather quickly. My Mothers friend Steve had come to help her. I loved Steve. I knew the moment I met him that he was a good man and I trusted him. I knew he would never hurt my Mom or make her cry. So I was always nice to Steve. He helped my Mom lift and carry to the van she had hired. I helped by carrying my balls. When the moving part was over, Steve returned to London and we had to go back to the old house to clean.

I couldn't help much, so I just lay there watching her and making sure the postman knew I had my eye him! I can't stand that bloody man. Every day he tries to break into my home by putting his hand through a hole in our door. I am fed up with him and he just doesn't learn. No matter how many times I bark, or try grab his hand through that hole, he is always back the next day!

I have lunged for him more times than I have had dog bones, and does the man learn? No! I really am sick of him.

So it was my job to keep watch while Mom was on her hands and knees washing floors, walls, cabinets, toilets, and whatever else she could find with her cloth and bucket. Then she painted the walls because she had hung pictures up and taking them down had peeled the paint off.

Finally it was all over and back in the car we got and drove to the mess waiting for us at our new home. First things first, my Mother and I went for a long walk on the Farm. Quite a while into our walk, we came across the farm manager who said 'it is soon going to be pheasant and grouse season, so please make sure Finley doesn't kill any birds'

I remember wondering what Pheasant and Grouse were. I had never killed anything in my twelve months of life. Why on earth would I do something like that? The man got back in his Land rover and he couldn't have been half way down the road, when I saw something moving in the hedges. I was off at full speed.

What the hell was that? I bolted into the hedges, back out, back in, I can see you, GOT YOU! I was as proud as punch. After belly crawling through the hedges, getting stuck in barbed wire, I had finally caught the escape artist. My Mom was going to be so proud of me. I went running back with my catch firmly held between my chompers and my tail wagging.

'Oh shit Finley! That is a Grouse. That is the very thing that man has asked me to keep you from Killing. Dammit man! Is it dead? Finley give that to me!'

She was seriously upset with me, and I was so proud of my catch. She took my trophy from my mouth and declared it dead. 'We have to bury the evidence Finley. For crying out loud don't kill any more of these or you will get us evicted before we have even unpacked'

After burying my catch of the day, we resumed our walk. I saw a few more of those tempting catches and chased them, but on pain of a death threat from my Mom, I never caught them. But I certainly did enjoy making them run for their lives and forcing them to fly into a tree. This was almost as much fun as chasing squirrels back at the last house!

This new home was proving to be a delight. I had Deer, Pheasant, Grouse, Rabbits, Squirrels, rats and random birds to chase. Wow this was a fun new life. I loved going for walks on this farm. So did my Mother to be fair. She would tell my Nan, that it freed her mind from day to day constraints.

It was a wonderful life. Looking back now, the short time we spent there, made up some of my most treasured memories.

Then one weekend, we had a visitor. I had heard my Mom on the phone again to my Nan saying 'James is coming over to visit. You remember James? Well he made contact and it looks like his marriage has ended so I invited him over. It's been years since I last saw him and to be honest, I could do with the company.'

Who the hell was James now? Urgh my whole rabbit chasing day had been ruined by this conversation. I had to just wait and see. Well he arrived later on the Friday afternoon much to Mothers delight. I on the other hand, could smell him from the time he stepped out the car and knew he was no good for her.

I was so unimpressed. I didn't like him one bit and I certainly didn't trust him. He was another Ryan, and my Mother couldn't see it. 'Hi James' she gushed.

'Hi gorgeous' He replied. Urgh, this was not good. She was making a very big mistake here.

So I did the only thing I know how to do well, and that is perform. I barked, and barked, I wouldn't go near him. He kept putting his stupid hand out to pat me and I would lift my lips showing him my teeth as a warning of what is coming next if he even touches me.

Poor Mom was in shock and didn't know what to do. She kept apologizing to this stupid James and saying 'Finley is not normally like this. Look he is not great with strangers. He is a bit skittish, but this behaviour I have never seen. He is genuinely upset.'

Damn right I was. She couldn't see and smell what I could, and she was walking into more heartache if she didn't wake up and listen to me.

It was hours of drivel I had to listen to. I was learning fast about humans and their oddities. He spent hours telling my Mother how much he had missed her and thought of her over the years. How he had secretly loved her all along. How he longed to have 'the dream' with her. Oh it was hours and hours of utter lies and nonsense. I was getting seriously pissed off with all this.

Finally my mother said she was tired and came downstairs with linen for James.

So, James ended up staying the night and sleeping on the sofa down stairs. I lay on the steps leading to my Moms room all night just in case this fool decided to follow her to our bedroom. I would make sure he didn't get very far. So I kept an all-night vigil.

Next day, his phone was going again, like it had all of the previous night and more lies spewed from his mouth. He never took a call while he was there and he made sure he never left his phone around either. I was so tempted to grab it out his back pocket and take it to my Mother. I just wish my Mother could see what I do.

I was a growing boy and my senses were developing very quickly. I was proving to be an excellent judge of character and she knew this. But James was her friend and so I believe she was just making excuses for him.

He left to go home, and we went out for a walk on the farm. I can't remember the exact amount of time but it was probably two weeks later, after James declaring undying love to my Mom that her phone rang in the early hours of the morning. I remember my Mom answering and saying 'what the hell are you talking about and who are you?'

Then she lay listening some more and then I heard 'Dear God! I have not been having an affair with James. He came over to my house a couple of weekends ago and spent the night on the sofa. I have never had sex with him and in fact I was under the impression he was single. Now you tell me he has been dating you for two years and you left your husband for him!'

I knew it! I told her!

Her and this very upset woman spoke for ages and turns out James is a player of note. He was caught having an affair with this woman, and several others behind his wife's back. Then he tried to have an affair with my Mother behind this woman's back. What a creep.

When she finally put the phone down, she looked at me and said 'You were right! He's a halfwit. Thank God I never slept with the prick! Let's get back to sleep Fin, he won't be coming over again, so you can relax!' Thank Anubis the dog God for that!

Come to think of it, all these years later, she chats to him via message maybe once or twice a year, but he never did come around again. He was very apologetic and begged my Mom's forgiveness, but it was over from that night on. That was a close shave.

But my dear Mother unbeknown to both of us at the time, was on a road to self-destruction. All through a lack of self-esteem and feelings of not good enough. This is what Steve had said and I had to agree with him. I didn't understand it all, but as life was unfolding and I was learning more and more about human beings and my Mother, I could see Steve had a point.

Ryan had broken my Mother. Years and years of put downs were showing themselves in her thoughts and actions. His constant chipping away at her self-esteem had led to self-doubt. Ryan was always judgmental, critical, intolerant, and never allowed her to have an opinion. So seldom did he show acts of kindness or empathy and Steve had called him a Narcissist.

She was in a dangerous place emotionally and as I have learned over time, having watched her and others and listening to countless conversations, it is not a safe place to be for humans. I was really concerned about her. I just wished she could love Steve like she did Ryan.

I never did understand why she couldn't just love Steve. He was such a wonderful man and so kind to my Mom and I. But she would say to my Nan

'I have known Steve for 25 years. I love him and he is my best friend. But I am sadly, not attracted to him. I feel no attraction for him at all. I can't bear the thought of anything physical'

Everyone loved Steve. There was never a person who met Steve that didn't love him the way we did. But whatever this physical attraction stuff was, it was a big problem for my Mother. So I had to give up the dream of Steve because my Mom was adamant. It was never going to happen. End of.

We had been in our new Farm Cottage for about 6 months when I heard we moving again. This time to a place called South Africa. I was guttered. I loved my farm and I loved our walks and now we were packing up again and by all accounts moving very far away.

This had all come about when my Moms, Step Mother died. She had put me into Kennels and had gone back to South Africa for the funeral. Something had happened on that trip and now we were moving there. I had no idea where it was or how far it was. All I do remember is it was a bloody long time in Kennels before she returned to pick me up.

What a fuss that proved to be. We had to sell up most of our belongings, and much to my horror, a lot of my balls went into the skip. She kept telling me she will buy me new ones once we get there, but these were my favourite ones. She did however pack my toy box in for shipping and I knew I had a couple of tennis balls in there along with fluffy toys and old bones which I had kept.

In the last 3 weeks before we left, so much was going on, that my Mom put me into Doggy Crèche during the day so she could work with no interference. That was fun actually. I got to play with so many dogs and I enjoyed myself. Problem with that, is we played on shale and it sliced my paw pads to ribbons.

I never complained, because I knew my Mom was busy and needed me out the way so she could work and pack. One evening, I was lying on my back with my legs splayed and my Mom noticed my paws. She was horrified. Back to the damn vet I went. Mom ended up buying me running shoes which were so cool. I was the envy of all the dogs.

I had to wear those every day when I left the house for two weeks to heal my puddies. It wasn't a problem, I actually found them really comfortable. Even Gordie my Nans Jack Russel and my friend thought they were way cool. During the last two weeks, Steve was with us almost every day, helping to pack and tidy up.

I heard her telling Steve that she had been offered a business opportunity from her ex-husband Owen, and that she felt it was an opportunity to set herself up that she couldn't turn down. Her, and Owen had got divorced something like 20 years ago but remained friends. She was sure it was the right move for us and Owen would not let her down.

I heard a lot about Owen in the build up to us leaving. I was skeptical, and not sure I was happy about this move. I was probably more on Steve's side. He would tell my Mom

'I am so happy for you. You will be fine. This is something you need to do Cheeky Monkey. You will find your answers and sort your life out' but with all the kind words, I could sense an underlying sadness.

He was not telling the truth and keeping his fears away from my Mom. Steve also knew Owen and that was a worry for me because I could sense Steve was not happy. Who was this man and was he another Ryan? I would find out soon enough.

Mom paid for a gold service which meant the vets came to our house to do all their pre-flight checks on me. They took blood, gave me injections, I got a passport with my photo in, I was now about to join the ranks of 'International Traveller' Wow, my real Mother would not believe this. Me, her son, going in an airplane and crossing three time zones. Gee I wished I could have shared all these experiences with her.

The time moved by very quickly and before I knew it, we had left the farm house and were staying with my Nan, Gramps and Gordie for the last two days before boarding. Gordie and I were the same age, eighteen months old. Gordie is a really cool dude. I like him very much.

We do have our scraps. It annoys me when he wants barking rights. If I hear a noise first, I react and he gets angry because I am barking. He says it's his home and he has the barking rights and not me. It's crazy. I am protecting my Mother and he says he is protecting his. So we argue a lot about who gets to bark and for how long, but all said and done, we get on very well.

Gordie is really very clever. He knows so much about so much. He is the one who told me about Anubis the Egyptian Dog God. He is a History buff. He told me my Nan and Gramps spend hours living in different centuries and researching everything. I have to be honest, some of the stuff he tells me just goes over my head. I am good with sussing out men and people in general. I know a lot about relationship problems and narcissist's, but Vikings, Saxons vs Celts, Romans and all that malarkey, not really.

Gordie watches TV and tells me about a bloke called David Attenborough. Honestly? I have heard my Mother mention his name and I know she watches the same stories on TV as Gordie, but truthfully, I can't be bothered most of the time.

I guess we can't all be interested in the same thing. But I knew I was going to miss him. I wondered if I would ever see him again. That last night, he let me have all the barking rights because he knew I was leaving the following morning. So that was really cool. He lay chewing on his stash of treats, and I protected my Nana's house.

Following morning, the travel van arrived to collect me. My mom was very emotional and so was my Nana. I was a bit scared to be fair but I had to be brave because my fear was affecting my Mother. When she said the usual 'See you in 5 minutes Fin' I knew it wouldn't be long and we would be together again.

She always said 'See you in 5 minutes' when she had to go somewhere and I wasn't going with in the car. I knew, 5 minutes meant she was coming back. Instinct told me this was going to be a long 5 minutes, but it didn't matter, I had, had a few long 5 minutes in the past, but she always came back and this time would be no different. So in the cage I stepped.

'I love you Finny. Be a good boy for me. NO biting! I will see you tomorrow in South Africa.' And with that, she turned away choking back her emotion and the van door was closed. I was on my way to London Heathrow. The 'no biting' thing is because I have a tendency to nip the people I don't like or trust. Especially if they come anywhere near my mom. But I would behave for her on that trip.

They drove me to a holding facility where more checks were done on me. My passport was checked, all my vet documents checked along with general fuss because I was leaving the Country. I was there for the day and that evening, I was transferred into a wooden crate. On the one side was the water bowl and on the other was my food. If you can call dry biscuits food!

I would have a word with her about the dry biscuits. My mom never fed me dry biscuits. She used to cook for me every night. Chicken, veg, rice and biscuits, Fish, or beef. I was not impressed with the Dog inflight menu, but thankfully it wasn't going to be long and I would eat a proper meal with my favourite veg Broccoli.

Then they sprayed something into my crate. What the hell it was I have no idea. I heard them saying it would calm me down for the flight ahead. Whatever it was, I can tell you it stunk and I didn't like the smell one bit, but it did make me a bit drowsy. That feeling I didn't like either. I am a Dog who likes to be in control and feeling dopey is not my thing. I have to be alert all the time. I am used to being on guard and now I was drugged and useless.

After that, it's all a bit of a haze really. I got driven to some other place at the airport and from there put on the plane. I noticed there were a few other dopey companions travelling with me in their crates. I wondered if they had dry biscuits on their Inflight Menu. I tried having a conversation with them, but none of them really made much sense.

The one dog Chichi I think her name was, was smaller than Gordie and that is small! All she could talk about was trips out in a designer pram or her mother's handbag. She spoke about things like fake tan, lipstick, different colours her nails had been painted, and how she was devastated that she wasn't allowed to be dressed for her flight. She felt naked. The humiliation at only being allowed to travel with her pink bow in her hair!

I had no clue what she was on about and thought that stinky stuff that they sprayed in our cage, must have affected her. I did chat briefly to some ugly looking dog. His face was scrunched up and his teeth seemed to be on the outside of his mouth. His name I forget now, but it was something like Bully.

This was his second trip to South Africa. He was born and grew up there, and his parents decided to move to the UK. After a couple of unhappy years, they had decided to return, so back he was going. I asked him a few questions about South Africa and what to expect. He said it was a cool place with great beaches and big gardens.

Beaches! I was happy about that, maybe my mom would take me to the beach again so I can swim and play with other dogs. Bully told me about dog fights he had been in but overall, it wasn't the longest conversation because that spray was making his words slur. Or was it his teeth on the outside of his mouth? I couldn't decide, but he was becoming more difficult to understand. Plus the engines had fired up and the noise was deafening.

I decided after that, to pretend to be asleep. The conversations were either boring, or difficult to understand. The noise from the engines had given me a huge headache. It was time for me to lie back now and wonder about the adventures that lay ahead for mom and I.

After what seemed like days to me, finally we were taken off the plane, put into another van and driven to another Veterinary Clinic. From there we were checked over to see that we were all OK and we were allowed to walk around, eat, poo, drink water and generally just spend a few hours outside of the crate.

I wasn't sure if this was South Africa, but I guessed it wasn't because I could understand no one. They all spoke a language I hadn't heard before. But hand signals and kind energies are universal. So I enjoyed my time. Chichi told me it was Dubai. A place her mother comes to shop. Who knows, the name rang a bell. I was sure that was the place my Mom had said I would be spending a few hours at before being sent on to South Africa.

I didn't care. The people were really nice to me. I knew I would see my Mom again because she had said '5 minutes' and I was just enjoying being able to walk around and stretch my legs. I was on my best behaviour and everyone thought I was so handsome. Plus the food on this stop was marginally better than the Inflight meal. We got to eat tinned dog food which wasn't the best, but at least it wasn't dried up biscuits.

Before I knew it, I was back in my crate, more of that stinky stuff was spayed into the crate and we were off to the next plane. I didn't see Chichi again. Maybe Dubai was her final destination. I never did ask. But I did see Bully with his teeth on the outside of his mouth along with a couple of other dogs that were new. In all, I think there were around seven of us on that flight to Durban, South Africa.

I remember I didn't bother talking much to any of the new travel companions. I kept to myself and decided sleep was the best option.

Next day, when the plane landed, I was taken to another holding facility and again a vet came to visit me and checked me over and gave me the all clear. I was put on my lead and allowed to walk around. It was then I heard her voice. My Mom was back, my 5 minutes was up. I was so happy. I have not wagged my tail that hard in a long time.

The lady holding me let me off the lead to run to my Mother. I literally jumped into her arms from joy. It was so exciting to see her and the relief I felt was immense. We were together again. Once I had calmed down, I noticed how hot it was. Man alive, I had not felt heat like this for ages. It was similar to the heat I experienced the first day my Mom saved me.

And there he was, the man called Owen. I wasn't sure about him. I would need to settle down a bit, and gather my wits about me before passing my judgement. On first appearance, he didn't smell too bad and I didn't pick up a bad energy. But I was tired, excited, and my senses were all over the place. I would get a good sniff of him later.

I was put in the back of his 4x4 and off we went. We arrived back at Owen's house which I must say, was rather impressive. He had the biggest house and garden I had ever seen. He had a swimming pool, and he had a miniature sausage dog called Milo who I instantly liked. Milo couldn't have been bigger than a 2 litre bottle of coke! He was slightly younger than me. He was a year old. Him, and I would be great friends. Milo welcomed me with open paws. I did sense a sadness in him, but we would talk about that later. For now, everything was new and there was so much to explore and sniff.

That first day, I also met Patricia, Owens house keeper and her two daughters. I instantly liked the little one Lizzy, she was probably Milo's age in human years so around seven years old and she would go onto to teach me to swim in the pool and we would have loads of fun including Milo into our games.

That night I lay outside with my Mom and Owen while they spoke about the business, drank beers, reminisced and laughed. Later when my Mom was tired and it was bed time, Owen shouted 'Milo, Finley, outside' I remember thinking, what? Outside? Is the man insane, I sleep on the bed with my Mother! Or at the least, on my Snoozzee next to her bed. I am not an outside dog. I live in doors! Beside all that, this place is scary.

Mom replied with 'Owen, Finley is an inside dog. He has just come off an almost 24 hour flight and this is all new to him. He will be so scared if he is left outside. I did tell you before I left that Finley is an inside dog and you agreed to him sleeping in the house. I am not happy to leave him outside on his first night in a foreign Country'

That was the first argument they had. Owen was not happy to leave me inside. Not only was I going to mess his house, but I was going to trigger his alarm system. In the end my Mother won, but there was a price to pay. She went to bed and I was left downstairs. Early hours of the morning, I could feel I needed a poo. I hadn't poo'd for going on two days and had to find my Mom and tell her to open up for me.

But the house was so big. It had five massive bedrooms, three bathrooms, two lounges, two dining rooms spread out over two levels and for the love of Anubis, I could not find my Mom. I was terrified and I couldn't ask Milo because he had been locked outside. I was so desperate and held onto my poo as long as I could and then I had to find a place I thought was safe and just let it all come out.

I was so ashamed of myself. I was taught never to wee and poo in the house. My Mom would be so disappointed in me when she sees this in the morning, but I really had no choice and I was sure she would understand that.

Following morning, unfortunately it wasn't Mom who discovered my poo, but Owen and he was furious. Later when my Mom came down the stairs he let her know in no uncertain terms his displeasure and that I was no longer allowed in the house because I poo'd on his wooden floor and I was responsible for dropping hair all over his house and my nails were scratching his solid wood flooring.

They had a terrible argument and it was then, that I ran outside and lay with Milo who was staying well away from Owen. That was when I learnt about Milo and of course Owen. Steve had been right to be concerned. This was all wrong and it was not going to end well.

Milo told me of his loneliness. He had been bought as a birthday gift for Owen's son David and after three weeks, no one wanted to know him anymore. The novelty had worn off and he was just a small dog who was getting in the way and who scratched the floors and was pretty much good for nothing.

He said he struggles with the large garden. It takes him ages to get from one side to the other. When he follows David down to his cricket practice net, he gets ignored and told to 'go away' He will get a pat on the head once in a blue moon, and just generally tries to stay out of everyone's way because he knows he is not wanted.

He said Owen often threatens to give him away if David doesn't start playing with him. But David is not interested. He said he can feel his time is up and he wishes he had a family that loved him like my Mom loves me. No one had spent any time teaching him anything. He had no stories to tell, he had been nowhere other than his garden, none of the visitors ever acknowledged him, he had a sad life and he hated sleeping outside because he said it's very scary for him.

The only time he ever got played with, was when on the odd occasion Lizzy and Patience came home from school and their Mom allowed them to swim and play in the pool. Milo would run around the edges of the pool barking and they would splash him with water. They sometimes allowed Milo in their hut which he enjoyed.

He also told me he didn't feel very well and rolled over to show me his belly. Under his very short and small arms he had this really bad skin disorder that he kept scratching. I felt so sorry for Milo. Here I was, so loved and protected. My Mother trusted me with her life and I her. We had the strongest connection and my Mom always put me first. My heart broke for Milo. I told him he should come and live with us, and he loved that idea but deep down we both knew it wouldn't happen.

He was unloved, misunderstood, scared, sick and ultimately a very lonely dog. I had to speak to my Mother about this. I had to show her Milo's rash. If I brought it to her attention, I knew she would do something about it. Milo's skin was rotting while he was alive.

That first morning, once the fight was over, Owen picked up his car keys and drove out through the electric gate. My Mom came outside onto the swimming pool deck to see what all the commotion was about. There she saw Milo and I were chasing around the edge of the pool barking at Lizzy and biting the water.

Mom loved watching us having so much fun but I looked up from the pool and she was teary and upset all over again. Gosh I remember being so angry. I hated seeing my Mom like this. I left Lizzy to swim alone and made my way to my Mother's side.

While she was sitting down, and although upset, I really did need to bring Milo's skin disorder to her attention. So I called him over. But Milo was now in a playing mood and was not allowing me to push him over with my snout. 'For the love of Anubis, Milo please! You must roll over so my Mom can see your belly. Just stop it now for a few minutes'

Even my Mom thought for a moment that I was bullying Milo. Silly dog. But he listened in the end and allowed me to push him onto his back. I made a point of sniffing Milo's belly while barking, and really showing my Mom something was wrong. 'Milo! Come here, what is that on your belly?' and she leant forward and picked Milo up to put him on her lap.

He was really good. He lay still on his back and allowed my Mom to have a good look. 'Thank you Finley for showing me this' she said and I just wagged my tail and gave a short bark in response. We had such a good communication. Although she didn't speak Dog and I couldn't speak Human, we understood each other very well.

'Milo, you need a vet my boy. This doesn't look good at all and it must be so painful. This is really awful. I am going to make an appointment with the vet down the road and get you sorted. You poor sausage.' Said my Mom. Milo just lay there on her lap with is little tail wagging and was enjoying the comfort my Mom was giving him.

Next minute the electric gate opened and in drove Owen again. Once he had dropped his keys in the kitchen and come back outside to continue the moaning at my Mom about me, she said to him 'Owen, Milo needs a vet. I have made an appointment for 14h00, It will cost around R700 (around £32 in real money) He has this awful skin disorder and it must be very painful.'

'Rubbish! I am not spending that amount of money on this dog. He is fine. I have some cream that I put on. There is nothing wrong with him. It's a normal heat rash' replied Owen.

Another fight ensued and this time, my Mother said 'Finley lets go. Milo, you can come with us, we going to the beach. I can't bear to sit here another minute' Oh boy it was only in effect day one of being in South Africa and things were going seriously wrong for us. I kept seeing Steve's face and remembering his concerned energy.

Anyway, with that, and while Owen was still arguing, we were in the car and heading out the electric gate. Milo was terrified. He had never left his house and although he loved my Mom, he was really scared.

'Milo, you need to relax. My Mom is taking us to the beach. You have no idea how much fun that is. You will love it, trust me please. Come stand next to me, the window is open and it will blow your ears back. It's such fun' I told him. Milo, joined me at the window and although he was too short to actually have his ears fully blown back, he could feel the breeze, it lifted the edges of his floppy ears and he could see the world passing by. He calmed down and agreed it was very exciting.

I will never forget that couple of hours with Milo on the beach. He ran and ran and rolled in the sand. He was in a world of his own. I kept calling him 'follow me, come to the water Milo!' but he was a bit scared of the waves. Come to think of it, so was I. This sea was different to the one we have back home. So I myself, didn't venture too far into it. I played in the shallow water and kept a close eye on Milo and Mom.

I saw my Mom pick Milo up and walk with him to the waters edge where I was playing. As the wave broke and the water thinned out, she put him down. He was barking and so excited. He ran through the water feeling safe because my Mom was right next to him and he knew if the water got out of control, my Mom would lean down and pick him up.

The fun we had. It was a wonderful experience for Milo and he kept thanking me for everything. Then it was time to go because he had to go to the vet.

The vet told my Mom that Milo must be in a lot of discomfort and that this was fungal and some kind of Dermatitis. I can't remember the name the vet said. It was a big word which I hadn't heard before and I didn't understand it. But the long and short of the story was my new friend had a painful skin disorder that was made worse from stress and heat.

He needed to be medicated immediately because this would spread across his whole body. Also because he is a sausage dog, he is very close to the heat on the ground and that he should be kept inside for a couple of weeks to allow his skin to heal. We all knew that was not going to happen. The vet gave Mom some cream and a two week course of antibiotics for Milo.

I remember my Mom paid with our money because rich Owen still refused to part with one cent towards Milo's ill health. Saying over and again, that it was not worth it.

Milo was so grateful to both of us. My Mom would lie him down on his back three times a day and rub this cream on his skin. Then give him his antibiotic and she gave Milo my Snoozzee bed to sleep on until she bought him a new one the following day. I didn't mind. Milo needed it more than I did. So I would just lie next to him and tell him some of my stories while he slept and tried to heal.

Unfortunately, things between my Mom and Owen just got worse by the hour. I was forbidden inside the house along with Milo. Which meant my Mom spent hours on end sitting outside with the two of us and sometimes Lizzy. She would phone my Nan, Harper and Jessica her long-time friends every day. Harper was mortified at how Owen was treating us. Mom, Harper, Owen and Steve had all known each other for decades.

I loved Harper. She was one of my favourite people. She had come on holiday to us in the UK when we lived with Ryan. Oh boy, that was another nightmare time because Ryan didn't like her and was not happy to see my Mom laughing and relaxing with her longtime girlfriend. Urgh, my mother, really does find them!

What I did know from listening to my mom talking, was that we would see Harper soon and that was very exciting for me. I couldn't wait for that to happen. She lived in Johannesburg.

The screaming and shouting was never ending. I remember Milo started healing. On day two he said to me he feels so much better and the pain is going. Every day when my Mom spoke to my Nan back in England she cried. This was really not good.

I heard her telling my Nan one morning 'Mom, my life is a complete fuck up. I left a secure job. A beautiful home, and all on the promise of a future and business with Owen. Thank God, I bought return tickets. Dear god! I should have known it was not going to work. Owen is not right in his head. He is just an arrogant, rich, control freak. I must have some kind of magnet on me that attracts all these dreadful men. I am going to the vet to sort Finley out and I am coming home. I can't do this anymore. We have only been here three days so I can't see there being a problem with returning to the UK. I will keep you posted'

Then she phoned the Farm back in England and was told our home is still available and if we back within a two weeks they will hold it for us and not rent it out. My Mom was over the moon and so was I on hearing that. It was looking good at that point.

I remember saying to Milo 'Oh thank Anubis for that! We going home! Milo you should see our home across the water. Maybe my Mom will take you with us and I will show you Rabbits, Grouse, Pheasants, Rats, and my all-time favourite, Squirrels! I have only been in this Country for three days and I have had enough. How you have lived with all this I will never know.'

Poor Milo didn't have a clue what I was talking about. He only knew dogs and birds. His general knowledge was extremely limited. He was just a dog that wondered around all day on his own and not a part of the family and because he was never spoken to, or taken anywhere, he knew nothing about anything.

The vet told my Mom I needed a Rabies Serology test. Unfortunately it would take three months for the results to come back because it was December and there was only one biological unit in the whole of Africa and it was closed until mid-January of the New Year. Mom was devastated. We were trapped. We had at least a three month wait before we could return. It was all a big mess.

Mom asked Owen 'Please can Finley and I just stay until I can sort out a return flight for us and he gets his Rabies Serology done and then we will leave. I will make sure that we both stay out of your way, but because it's 7th of December, I can get nothing done until mid-January'

Owen's reply? 'No! I want my house back. I have a woman I want to date and you will just be getting in the way and making things uncomfortable. Plus I am sick of Finley's hair and now Milo sleeps in the kitchen and I will have to break him out of that habit too. No you can't stay. I am prepared to drive you and Finley to your Father in Witbank and that is where my responsibility ends'

What a prick. Here was a man who lived on his own in a humungous home, and he couldn't even give my Mom who he had not only been married to, but had known for more than 25 years, one room. Shameful. Steve would never had done this to Mom.

There was so much drama. I remember wondering how on earth we were ever going to get out of this mess. My Mother was in a state because she didn't want to go to her Father. They did not get on, and could only really spend hours together before things started turning sour.

I met Adam and Ann when I was still a puppy. Maybe about 5 months old and they came over on holiday and stayed with us. I didn't really remember much about him and couldn't remember his smell. I was too young at the time. But listening to the things my Mother was saying, I wasn't sure I wanted to get to know him at all!

She was desperate to find a way for us to leave South Africa, but sadly the odds were not in her or my favour. She did ask Owen if she could take Milo which was amazing, but Owen told her she was bloody mad and why on Earth would he give her Milo. She begged Owen to please keep up with Milo's daily creaming and his antibiotics because he still had several days to go.

Also explaining to him, that Milo needed shade and coolness to heal. The kitchen was not in his house per se, and allowing Milo on his new dog bed, to just rest in the cool of the kitchen was not going to cause Owen any hardship.

Also the kitchen had slate flooring and not his precious wood flooring. It was the kind and humane thing to do.

Owen's reply 'There are plenty cool places he can lie outside.' I guess the day he drove us out, he told his Servant to put poor Milo back outside into the African heat and who knows if Milo did ever finish his treatment. It would be over two years before I listened to a phone call between Mom and her girlfriend Harper, that not long after we left Owen's, Milo was outside, Owen didn't see him, and he reversed his 4 x 4 over Milo, killing him. I cried for my little friend.

He had such a horrible life and it ended so tragically. I will always remember that little dog and the joy we shared at the beach and the wind blowing his ears in the car. At least we brought a bit of love and light into his life for the few short days we spent with him. I hope he is well in dog heaven and that Anubis kept a special place for him.

Chapter 4

The car was packed with my Mom and my stuff. A lot of it was chucked in black plastic bags and my Mom found a space for me in the back of the 4 x 4 where she lay my bed down and a window was opened for me. I said my goodbyes to Milo and Lizzy, Mom gave Milo a big hug and kiss and told him she hoped he got better soon and thanked him for playing with me for the few days we were at Owen.

So much had happened in all our lives in five short days, it was difficult to get my head around. We must have lived a year within those five days. I could only imagine what my Mom was going through. I was sweating my coat off in the back of that car. The sweat was dripping off my snout! It was a long drive. I think it took us around six hours to arrive at my Grandad, Adam's house.

It wasn't long after arriving at Adam when I realized why my Mom did not get on with her Father. Also it would not be long before I would miss the drama of being at Owen. With all the upset we went through in those five days with Owen, things were about to get so much worse for both of us.

The car stopped. My Mom climbed out and let me out the boot. Owen heaped all her bags just inside Adam's gate, turned around, said 'Bye Danny, good luck and I am sorry things turned out the way they did' climbed back in his car, and off he drove. Unbelievable stuff for me to witness.

I was trying really hard not to be biased but I really didn't get a good scent from Adam. He was a hard man, a bully, and a man with little compassion and empathy. Also he was another one, who knew so little about how to treat dogs. I was very disappointed with the people I had met so far.

The first few hours after we arrived were really very confusing for me. I didn't know what was going on and I was trying to follow my Mothers conversation but it wasn't easy. From what I could make out, her Step Mother, Ann had died six weeks earlier, so that must have been when she put me into kennels and went to a funeral. It was making sense now. The woman that we saw sitting outside when we arrived, was Adam's new Fiancée. He told my Mom he was in love and that they were getting married in six weeks' time.

Mom was not impressed. She said something along the lines of 'Jesus Dad, Mom's body is not even cold and you getting re married? You must have been having an affair with this new woman behind your dying wife's back!' Ann by all accounts, had died from cancer and had died a very lonely death. Turned out, that he had met Esme on a dating website.

To be fair, I actually liked Esme. I didn't get a bad smell from her. I know my mother was very upset, and the tension was thick in the air, but I didn't mind her. Whatever her sins were, I thought she smelt just fine. It was the first person since I had arrived that I had been comfortable being around and who had a kind energy.

That first day from memory, was bloody awful. My Grandad hadn't even prepared a room for my Mother and like Owen, he wanted me to sleep outside.

'Dogs belong outside! My dogs never, ever, came inside. They were only ever allowed to lie by the door and if they ventured further into the house, I would use the sjambok on them. They were disciplined animals. This Finley, needs a good sjambok. If he growls at me one more time, he will be very sorry'

Adam had two sjamboks on his wall. A sjambok for those of you who don't know, is a heavy leather whip, traditionally made from adult hippopotamus or rhinoceros hide. It's carried by many South Africans for self-defense. My mom told me that.

The reason I growled at him, was because I just didn't trust him. He kept calling me over, but I could sense his intense dislike and I felt he would hurt me. I was very uncomfortable in this new house and I was also picking up on my Moms fear. But I knew she would protect me from Adam, so I tried to lighten up a little. I played ball with Esme, and I allowed Adam to scratch my ears.

Although he was really mad at my Mom, he buckled and allowed me to sleep inside the room with her. The sofa and other chairs and beds were strictly out of bounds. Which was fine by me. As long as I got to sleep with my Mom, I was happy.

That first night would be the start of the next forty one days of pure hell for both of us. When I look back on those days, my whole body shudders. My hair stands on end and my paws prickle. But we got through it, otherwise I wouldn't be writing this book and telling you my story.

So I will try and remember all the things that happened in the days until we left! You know what it's like, when you live through a very stressful situation, your brain just seems to go blank. It's like you blocked it out or buried it so deep.

First of all, let me say, I didn't actually mind Witbank during the day. Mom and I would go for long walks and we both enjoyed our time out of the house. My Mom was using Ann's old car and her and I would venture out. One of our first visits was to Harper who lives in Benoni which with moving traffic, is about an hour's drive away.

It was amazing for me to see her again. I was all over her and she was laughing. Every time she dove into the pool, I would jump in after her. Bonus was she had five cats I loved chasing. OK! I am not a cat killer! I just enjoy the chase. From my earlier growing up experience with cats, I don't like them, but I did have my only friend in those days Barney. You remember me telling you about Barney.

So what type of dog would I be, if I was a cat killer after my best friend was a cat? Harper wasn't happy all the same because apparently one or two of her cats were really old. I had to calm down with the cats because I was getting into trouble. But we had such fun at Harper.

Another great memory I have of Witbank was a weekend away to a Farm on a big lake. It was a friend of my Mom and he and his wife had invited my Mom and me, can you believe that? I was so happy. When we arrived there, I couldn't believe my eyes. It was like a sea of water. I got to swim, go in a boat, chase a cat up a tree, and I've never shared this before, it's humiliating, but I got chased by a demon black cat. I was terrified of that thing. I won't even tell you the threats it made to me. That cat had a filthy mouth!

But the weekend we spent there is one of my few good memories of Witbank times. Other times and on days when Mom and Adam were getting on, Mom would take me to the pub with Adam while they had a couple of beers. I didn't mind those outings either, but there were so many people whose smell I really didn't like. So I would eventually end up barking at them and getting into trouble. But at least I was with my Mom, so all was good.

It was night time in Witbank that I didn't like. I gradually got used to Adam. I still didn't like him, and I certainly didn't trust him or want to be alone with him, but he kept his distance and I kept mine. I tried my best to stay out his way and became my Mothers shadow. I wouldn't let her out of my sight. Which used to really irritate Adam. He often said 'Leave your bloody Mother alone! What is it with this dog, that he follows you everywhere?'

Fortunately, he began going away quite often to spend time with Esme in some city called Pretoria. So Mom and I were left on our own in the house and it was so very scary. Witbank at night is just awful. My Mom walked everywhere at night with a gun. I think it was a 38 special. Can't remember, but that gun went to the toilet with my mom and slept on the pillow next to her.

I used to be on guard 24/7. I just never really had time to rest. I was watching Adam, watching my Mom, watching out for burglars, and people wanting to generally do us harm. My nerves were shot.

I used to always feel so guilty asking her to go out for a wee or poo at night. I could sense her fear and I knew myself it was very dangerous to open up. Word by now, would have got out that we were alone in the house, but what could I do? I need to wee and poo. So Mom would open up with the gun loaded and ready to fire just to let me do my business.

Then back inside we would come and everything got locked and bolted. I remember she hated Adam's lounge because his curtains didn't close. She used to say to my Nan, Jessica and Harper 'Who the hell has curtains that don't close and are just for show? Dammit man, I feel like I am living in a gold fish bowl. I'm bloody terrified and can't live with the lights off all night just so I can see what's going on outside!'

My Nan told her to take sheets and drape them over the windows for privacy. So that is what she did. She had sheets hanging everywhere, which had to quickly be unhooked, folded and put back in the cupboard before Adam returned home from his visit to Esme.

Thing is with Adam, he was always putting my Mom down. Nothing she really did was good enough. Adam was very much a man's man. We get that in the dog world too which is how I recognized it. Not to say they don't like girls, but some dogs I have met on our walks, have said they prefer male dogs company. Myself? I love the girls.

Adam was always grumpy, and he drank a lot. When he drank, it could go one of two ways. Either he was overly nice, or overly horrible. He had terrible mood swings. He could be aggressive at the flick of a switch. I did pick up early on though that he was sick. Sadly only I could pick that up. There was no way of telling my Mom. Unlike Milo who I really liked and who I could talk to and explain he had to roll over so I could make a big deal of sniffing his belly so my Mom would look, it was difficult with Adam.

I couldn't exactly roll him over and give him a once over. I would have to sniff his whole body, but from the times he passed out on the lounge chair, and I got close enough to him without him waking up, my guess it was something in his head. But it was a guess because there were other areas that didn't smell quite right either. My mother mistook my smelling of Adam when he was asleep as me warming to him. Absolutely not! I was terrified of the man at the best of times. His personality could change in a nanosecond.

During the day and after our morning walk, my Mom would job hunt. She had to get back into the Shipping Industry. She would say she needed to earn money or we were never getting out of here. Oh and in case you wondering, she did ask Adam for help financially to get home, but he refused. He said he had waited a long time for her to come 'home' and that she must 'stop your bloody nonsense. You ARE home! Your Mother has had you all these years, it's now my turn'

It was so strange for me. I could sense he did love her, and he did want her there, but his difficult, aggressive personality did nothing to improve their relationship. Funny how such a clever, well-educated man, can get it so completely wrong. But I guess that is a human for you. Or maybe it was that ill smell I kept picking up. Who knows?

He did end up buying her a laptop for Xmas so her job hunting would be made easier. She was very grateful. She started out looking for work in Witbank but the salaries were so small and the work so limited. She did go for a few local interviews but nothing really came of them.

Having the laptop was cool because when Adam was out, we would Skype my Nan and Gordie. I would bark hello to Gordie from the back ground. It was so wonderful for me to have a quick barking conversation with Gordie. It didn't last long because Mom and Nan were trying to talk about our situation and Nan would shout 'Gordon! Quiet!' and on this side, my Mom would be shouting 'Finley! Stop it!' but we at least got to exchange a few words every time they Skyped.

Mind you saying that, Gordie would take any opportunity he had to bend my ears about the latest documentary he had watched with my Nan and Gramps. I love Gordie, but man alive can that dog bang on about boring stuff.

Adam's sister, Aunty Amelia arrived for a few days over Christmas which was nice. I liked her too. She had a great smell and I enjoyed lying on her feet in the lounge. Adam of course, always had some sarcastic comment to pass, but for the few days Aunty Amelia was there, it was enjoyable. She seemed to have a calming effect on her brother.

All too soon, she had to return to Durban and it was once again, Adam, Mom myself, and the gun!

I remember there was so much tension between my Mom and Esme whenever she came over to stay a few days. Mom was very upset because her step mother's personal items were being given to Esme and not her one living son Luke. She had the biggest fight with Adam over that. They were screaming at each other and she said to him 'You have no right to give

Mom's stuff to this new woman. Her son and her grandchildren are the people who should be taking everything Mom left behind. You a selfish bastard'

His reply was always 'I fucking paid for everything, therefore it is mine to do with what I like, and I am giving it to Esme. Don't you dare talk to me like that again, or I will use the sjambok on you my girl. Don't think you too old for a hiding!' Even though at that point my Mom was forty seven years old.

I used to listen to her talking to Harper and Jessica and of course my Nan. She always said it was incredibly wrong of Adam. Luke and his wife were so poor and struggling every day to put food on their table. She had two step brothers but one had died many years ago, leaving only Luke. But for some reason, Adam felt he had done enough for Luke over the years and that he was under no obligation to give him one photo off the wall.

They by all accounts, were poor whites in Africa and I believe there are many of them. My mom used to tell everyone how expensive South Africa is and her heart was very sore over Luke and his family, but there was nothing she could do. Nothing. Adam was a stubborn, head strong man, and his word was law.

Well he was a Lawyer, so I guess that made sense. I didn't really understand all this but if it upset my Mother then it upset me. I was learning so much about people and their emotions, their selfishness, their greed and their totally messed up sense of morality. We don't have that in our world.

I remember the one day, my Mom was furious. Esme came over and Adam had told her to go around the house and mark with post it notes, what furniture she wanted and what she didn't. He was planning on moving in with Esme into her by all accounts, beautiful, fully furnished house.

Esme was walking around 'I'll have this, let's take that, Oh! I will find a place for this and I don't like that.' yet in the next village Luke was sitting with scraps! One of the things Esme chose was a beautiful old chest. Once Esme had left my Mom asked Adam about the chest.

'Oh that was Ann's, Mothers chest. She gave it to Ann when we got married. It's beautiful don't you think?'

Again my Mom said 'Dad, please, you cannot give this to Esme. Please I am begging you, give it to Luke. It was his Grannies chest and it belongs to him. Please do not give this to Esme. It is not yours to give away'

Urgh more screaming and fighting between them. Remembering this, the chest never did make it to Luke. I believe Esme still has the chest. We did a lot of walking in those days. We were always pounding the pavements just so my Mom could get some air and time alone. I didn't mind. I learned so much about a dog's life in South Africa from those walks.

I began to understand what a dog's position is in this Country. Most of these dogs were not pets. They had one purpose and that was to attack anyone who came into their yard irrespective of race.

Most of them had never seen the inside of their house, and pretty much all of them had never been taught about life, been spoken to, or befriended by their owner. They were angry, aggressive dogs who swore a lot and who wanted nothing more than to find a way out from their yard to re arrange my pretty face.

They were fed, watered and that is where it ended. It was a reality that was so foreign to me. All the dogs I knew back home had different lives completely.

Even if they did have big gardens, they were always walked and we would all meet on the pitch and have a good ol catch up. But these dogs, had never left their yard. All very strange and a lot of them had been beaten on more than one occasion. There were so few exceptions to this.

I grew ever more grateful for the home I had ended up in and having the Mother I do. Gosh I had it good. I almost felt guilty listening to some of the painful stories I was told while walking on the pavements.

We came across one dog whose owners had gone on holiday and left it alone in the garden. They left it with no food or water that was visible and this dog told me he was so hungry. I don't remember his name, but he said he had resorted to eating plastic bottles, grass, mud, and anything else he could find because there was nothing to eat.

My ever alert mom, on walking past this dog two or three times, and seeing him always in the same spot and never seeing any life from the house or yard, began feeding it. She phoned the RSPCA and spoke to neighbours who all said the family always does this. They just up and go on holiday and leave the dog to its own devices.

They had all at some point, chucked biscuits into the yard. My Mom managed to push two bowls through the gate and every day we would go there with food and she would use a coke bottle to fill up the water bowl. This dog had some horrifying stories of brutality to share with me.

He had been beaten and had more bones in his body broken than I had, had dinners. He was fearful of everything and everyone. They would tie him up and let the kids beat him with sticks and kick him. They believed it would make him more vicious and he would be a better guard dog.

On the odd occasion he was also used in dog fighting to strengthen his character. That explained some of the dreadful scars he had on his body.

You know, I guard my Mother with my all. I would put my life on the line for her and that loyalty and utter devotion, is because of the love and good care I have received. How do people get it so wrong? How do humans live with themselves? I just don't get it. As in the human world, if you nice to someone they usually nice back to you. It's the same in the dog world. Why would it be any different?

We have a heart that beats like humans do. We have emotions. We have fear. We have joy. We have trust and distrust. We have a sixth sense. We bleed red blood if we cut or hurt. We pine for our loved ones. We mourn a death. We get sick. We grow old. We get arthritis. We get ill sometimes. We have good days and bad days. We feel pain whether it be emotional or physical. We dream. We smile. We just like humans in so many ways, so why do they get it so wrong? I don't think I will ever understand or get the answers to that.

So those walks for me, were also very interesting and sad at the same time. My Mom was starting to go for interviews which I hated. It meant I was left alone with Adam. I used to pray to Anubis that she would be quick and not leave me with him for too long.

When she left, I would run to her bedroom and curl up on the bed to stay out of his way. On the days he was home, as her car left the driveway, he would come into the room and shout 'Get out! Fucking dog. I will teach you some manners. You a dog, OUTSIDE!' and I would move as quickly as I could outside and find a tree to lie under and stay very still.

My Mom never knew this because when she arrived home and saw me outside, she assumed it was because that is where I wanted to be. Adam would never tell her anything. So my trauma no one saw except Adam, his servant and myself. Also my Mom didn't know that Adam had given the servant permission to hit me if I barked at her. 'Hit him with the sjambok or the broom' that was the instruction.

It was very tough being at Adam. When he was there it was mostly awful and when he wasn't there it was always awful because my Mom was glued to her gun. Her fear on those days would run through my veins. She was right to be fearful. Every night without fail, there was danger lurking outside. I could sense it. Smell it. I would put my deepest bark on and do my best to scare them away.

I honestly think it worked because we never got attacked in the house. Our neighbour on the right got held up at gun point and robbed. Our neighbour on the left, got held up and in the end shot. Yet somehow, my Moms God and my God Anubis seemed to protect us. Almost cloaking our house in an invisible protection.

Then one day my Mom had another interview in Johannesburg. This she told me is a big one. 'Finley if I get this job, in a few months' time, we out of here. Pray for me boy and please be a good boy while I am away. I am going to be gone several hours because it's an hour's drive there, then the interview and another hour to drive back here. That's if there is no traffic. Stay out of Adam's way. Wish me luck boy'

'Dad I am leaving for my interview. Please do not pick on Finley or make his life miserable while I am gone. My interview is at 11h00 so I should be back all going according to plan, around 14h00 the latest.' She said and he replied with something like 'You and this fucking dog. Good luck with your interview and don't bloody speed. Watch these roads and keep your eyes open. Don't be a dumb blonde or you will wind up dead. Stay alert. This is not the UK. People get hijacked and shot daily on that road you travelling. Do not stop for anything or anyone. Do you hear me? Forget about your bloody dog for once'

She called me over and whispered in my ear 'Finley, I am sorry. But if I don't go, I won't ever get a job and we will never get back home. Please my boy, stay out of his way. I love you. I will see you in 5 minutes' and off she went.

Having learnt from the last time, and not wanting to risk anything, I didn't even go near my Mothers bedroom. I ran straight outside and I lay under that tree until she returned. I didn't even go for a wee or a poo. If I lay quietly, and didn't move a muscle, hopefully he would leave me alone, which on this occasion, thankfully he did. My Mom took all day to come home. She was so much longer than she said she would be. This was a long 5 minutes. I was beginning to panic and really needed a wee but still didn't want to move, when I heard her car drive through the gate. Thank Anubis she was home. I could relax. She would tell me why she had taken so long.

Turns out, she had the best interview ever and the company had offered her an amazing opportunity. All her years of living in the UK were now paying off. She knew the UK market in the Shipping Industry like the back of her hand and they were going to pay her a lot of money to open up a company in Durban, KwaZulu-Natal for them.

She was so excited and kept saying 'Thank you god' and in turn, I kept saying 'Thank you Anubis' we were finally going to get out of here. I couldn't wait. I would move to a dump with my Mother, anywhere but here, was good for me. She hugged me hard and said 'Finny foo, we moving to Durban and back to the sea. Sorry my boy for being so long, but it was an incredibly long interview.'

I remember being so excited. Durban! Wow! Maybe I would see Milo again and we could check on his belly. In reality, I never saw Milo again and my Mother never spoke to Owen again. She had bolted that door shut and nothing in the world would open it again. Her bitterness and pain ran too deep. I can understand that.

Adam congratulated her and asked her how she planned on getting to work and back every day while she lived over an hour's drive away. Shit, I hadn't thought of that. Dear God, I would have a whole day alone and have to stay safe from Adam. Oh this was not so good after all.

She told her Dad that she would get up really early. Try be on the road for 06h30 to be at work by 08h00. She would also speak to her new boss about leaving an hour earlier every day to miss some of the traffic and she would be back in Witbank by 18h00. That was going to be twelve hours a day alone. My heart sank. I knew I should be happy for her, but she had no idea what I went through every time she left me alone.

They ended up arguing about the wear and tear she would be putting on Ann's car and it ended with 'What do you plan to do with this bloody dog while you gone?' The man was truly incorrigible.

'Dad, I have to leave Finley here. I can't very well take him to work with me and there is no one else I can leave him with.' And he replied 'What about that friend of yours in Benoni? Can't she have this dog while you working?' Mom said she would speak to Harper which she did and Harper apologized but said she is in and out all day. She ran a business from home which meant lots of strangers in and out. She couldn't be responsible for my safety. Plus, I chased her cats.

Mom was stuck. She had no choice but to leave me in Witbank at Adam's mercy. Boy was I sorry I had ever tried to play with her cats. Now look. I had created a rod for my own back.

That following week was the worst week of my entire life and one which scarred me mentally, physically and emotionally for a very long time.

Mom went shopping for clothes in the days building up for the following week. Stuff she could wear for work. She had a very senior position and she explained she needed to look the part. I didn't mind that because she took me in the car with her and left me on the back seat with the window almost down in the underground parking lot while she shopped.

I made sure no one came anywhere near our car. If there was one thing I was really good at, was keeping my mom and our stuff safe. I was on red alert while she shopped.

All too soon, it was Monday 17th January and she had to go to her new work. As she had planned, she was up before the sun rose and getting ready to leave

'Finley, I will only be back tonight. It's going to be an incredibly long day for you. Stay out of Adam's way and I will be back in 5 minutes OK? Love you my boy'

After ruffling my hair and kissing my hooter she was off. It was another horrible day without her. I think Adam was jealous of the relationship I had with his daughter. He honestly didn't understand how a dog can be so close to a human. It was a world he had never existed in and one he wanted to control and couldn't.

A friend of his came over that day to visit and he was telling Mike the story about how I was lacking in discipline and how he had used the sjambok on his two previous dogs who had by now died. The last one dying a few months ago.

He said she had come into the house and made it to the dining room before collapsing. Initially when he saw her, he shouted for her to footsack. Which is a Dutch slang word for 'get out' and when she didn't move, he went and got the sjambok, believing she was defying him. Just before he brought it down on her, he realized there was something very wrong and that she was not defying him but, dying. She had crawled into the house to die.

He was not happy to put her in his car, and she subsequently died on the way to the vet. Yet he told Mike how much he loved his dogs and how they meant the world to him. They had been German Shepherds and according to Adam, obedient, disciplined and they knew their place! Unlike me of course.

I remember that day being damn long and I spent pretty much all of it, under my tree and only really came out when I was thirsty or needed a quick wee. My 5 minutes were eventually up and I heard my Moms car up the drive way. Boy was I happy and also so hungry.

As soon as I ran through the house to wait at the front door, Adam shouted 'Hey!' muttering under his breath, 'fucking dog' and continued with 'OUTSIDE!' but I didn't listen. I could hear the keys and knew he could do nothing, my Mom was just about the open the door and if she caught him hurting me, there would be trouble. He knew this and I knew this. So I stayed where I was and was the first person to greet her.

This small defiance would turn out to be my last against Adam.

That evening Mom explained to Adam while I lay at her feet, that she now realized the travelling in and out every day was not going to work. 'I told you!' He interjected. She had been held up on that highway with tyres burning, and a full out gun fight. She went on to say that Harper had offered for her to stay every other night in Benoni. Something like a Monday and Wednesday. My Moms office was only a ten minute drive from Harper's house and it would make things a whole bunch easier for her.

I understood this. Believe me I did. At first I thought I was going with, but I was wrong. Harper still didn't want me to stay there because of strangers coming in and out and of course her cats.

How I regretted ever chasing those cats. Even though my Mom knew I would never hurt one, Harper was taking no chances. My fate was sealed. Oh and in case you wondering where Steve is in all this. Well Steve, how did my Mother put it? Ah yes 'was swanning in Mauritius' She used to say Steve lived the dream.

He had loads of money and he did help us out many times in those first few months and Mom was in touch with him almost daily. Along with Harper, Jessica and my Nan. He also offered to pay for Mom to fly to Mauritius for a few weeks to get away from Witbank and help her to clear her mind. He used to say 'come and get some sun on your back, chew on some prawns by the sea cheeky monkey. Sip on a cocktail and together we will work out a plan for you and Fin' again, she had no one to leave me with so she thanked him but turned the offer down.

After hours of talking, it was decided that my Mom would stay at Harper for the next three nights. So that meant, Tuesday, Wednesday and Thursday and she would return back to Witbank on Friday after work.

She really didn't want to leave me and even asked her boss if she could bring me to work with her. She was truly worried for my safety. However hours later talking to her Dad, and with him assuring her over and over 'Danny, your dog will be fine. I won't hurt your bloody dog! Go and do your job and stop all this fussing over Finley, it's insane. He is a dog and you have a bloody life to sort out, so stop your bullshit now'

The arrangements had now been agreed upon. Tonight was the last night I would see her until Friday. How I prayed everything would be OK. I knew it wasn't going to be easy with Adam, but I had learned that if I stayed out his way, he generally left me alone. So that was my plan. Spend as much time as possible, under my tree with my ball, and out of his way and hopefully Friday would come quickly.

Following morning was Tuesday, she was up early and packed a little bag. I lay on the bed watching her and could sense she was unhappy. 'Finley, I really am sorry my boy, but I cannot do this drive every day. It's like running the gauntlet. It's dangerous for a woman on her own. You a target the minute you on that highway.

I am staying at Harper for the next three nights and then I will be home. Next week, I will stay away two nights so it's a little easier on you. Stay out of Adam's way. Don't bite anyone, and remember I love you. I will know if something is wrong. You and I have a good connection. Call me in your mind. OK? I will be back in 5 minutes.'

And off she went. It was horrible. I cried and cried and that was the first of my mistakes. Adam was thoroughly pissed off because I howl like a wolf when I am in emotional pain. He charged at me and told me to 'Shut up! Or I will shut you up'

So I took myself to my tree and lay there quietly. He was going out to work and told the servant 'If that bloody dog gets in your way, you sjambok him. You do a good job today, I want that ironing finished by the time I get home, and don't eat all my bloody bread, and don't use my sugar in your tea. I have left your bread on the counter. You don't eat my food, do you hear me? I want these floors clean, and you never move the bloody sofas, move them! You a bloody lazy bitch, you must work hard today. That is what I pay you for'

Urgh he was such a bully and this woman I could see, was not only terrified of him but the smell I got was pure hatred. She felt like I did only she didn't have a tree to hide under and she had a family to feed so she had to put up with his nonsense every day. Many times I had heard my Mom saying to him 'Dear God Dad, you truly are horrible. How can you speak to people like this? She is terrified of you and you are nasty. Everyone feeds their servants when they come to work. Why is your house keeper not allowed to use some of the sugar in her tea? You really are a mean man'

His reply was always the same 'she is a bitch and cannot be trusted. She will take the fucking gold out my teeth and steal me blind given half the chance! You don't know what you talking about. Stop interring in my fucking home. As for the sugar, she uses half my fucking pot of sugar in one cup of tea. I am not having that.'

My Mom was horrified. She called her father a racist and evil man. Saying one day he would be punished for his behaviour and the way he treats people. Mom said his servant was a human being just like him. She was a mother, a daughter, a sister, a cousin, an Aunty, she meant a great deal to someone and many people loved her. To be honest, Adam treated most people irrespective of race and including his own daughter with nothing but harsh words, insults and disdain. That my Mom said did not make it acceptable.

So after the servant whose name I truly cannot remember, had been instructed to sjambok me if I got in the way, and warned not to eat or drink his food, he left. The relief was immense for me. I walked outside, drank some water, played with my ball a bit, and mostly spent the day under my tree because it was extremely hot.

That first day went by with no issues to really speak off. The servant got everything done and was waiting for Adam to come home and pay her so she could buy food for her family and get home with a taxi. I stayed out of her way, and never gave her a hard time at all.

I heard Adam's car arriving and didn't move. He came inside 'Where is that bloody dog?' he asked. She replied with 'outside boss' with that, he relaxed, paid her the money and she walked out. Now I faced the evening with him alone.

I stayed outside, while he poured himself a whisky. I could smell that he had already had a few of them before arriving home, but that was Adam. He drank a lot of whisky every day and this day was proving to be no different. 'Come here Finley, come and sit by your grandad' he called. Ah, this was the softer mood. As I said before, some days the whisky made him aggressive and others, it made him really nice.

I was scared to go over to him because I knew what lay beneath that niceness, but I also didn't want to cause any trouble, so I slowly walked over with my head hung down and sat next to him. He was talking to me for hours. He forgot all about feeding me because the whisky had taken over.

He told me about his army days. How he missed Ann. Then how much he loved Esme. In the next breath he was saying how he had never loved a woman like he had my Nan. Then I heard about a woman he had bought a flat for in town and furnished. This woman he was having an affair with behind both Ann, when she was alive, and now Esme's back.

But he loved her too! He went on for hours about how much he loved my Mom and how she always misunderstood him and how he saved her life when she was a baby by doing a blood transfusion with reeds. What a good Father he had been. How unappreciated he felt. How my Mom had loved her Step Father more than she did her own flesh and blood.

All the while he was stroking me and was being really very nice. My stomach was grumbling and I was really hungry, but Adam had now passed out in his chair. So I took myself to my Moms bed. I lay thinking of the things he had been talking about.

I remembered old conversations between my Mom and Nan about how Adam is a Walter Mitty. He had elaborate fantasies about his life which were untrue, and he rewrote History to suit himself. More than half of what came out his mouth was utter nonsense. He was also a renowned cheater on his wives and girlfriends. I remembered my Nan telling my Mom that when she was married to Adam he used to lock her in the flat when he left for work.

If he didn't like the food she had cooked, he would throw the plate of food against the kitchen or dining room wall. The one night he had a gun to my Nans head and made her swallow her wedding ring. My Nan also went to his office unexpectedly one day to find him with his secretary on his lap and his hands all over her breasts. The marriage between him and my Nan only lasted two years.

I believe he had also hit all the woman in his life. Well, to be fair, I could believe that very easily because I knew more than anyone, the aggression that lay in him. I could sense it. As for my Moms, Step Dad, well she had always said he was a wonderful father. He brought her up and was the best Dad a girl could have wished for.

I'm sure I remember her telling me, she only met Adam for the first time at the age of fourteen, not much older than me and it was a disaster. They had gone on to have a very difficult relationship. I was remembering all these conversations and must have fallen asleep.

I woke up thinking, well, I have survived Tuesday. I just need to get through two more sleeps and my 5 minutes is up and my Mom will be home. But I was so hungry. I knew my Mom had left my dog biscuits in the kitchen, and I wondered if I couldn't open that packet and get something to eat. It was now Wednesday and the last time I had eaten was on Monday evening when Mom fed me.

So while Adam was in the shower, I ventured through to the kitchen and realized it would be impossible. It was a zip lock bag and yes, I could tear it open, but that would cause even more trouble. I would have to wait. Maybe he would remember today to put some biscuits in my bowl. So I made my way back to the bedroom. If I slept some more, maybe the hunger pains would go away.

I heard the gate bell go. There was an intercom at the gate leading to house. When that went and my Mother was here alone, it was red alert time. It was always someone who was either looking for a job, wanting food, asking for money or had bad intentions. Adam told my Mother to never just open the gate. Never walk up to the gate to talk to anyone, it was extremely dangerous. You had to talk through the intercom. Even though it was not my house, it was my duty to protect it, and the people inside which was Adam on this morning.

I ran through to the lounge to the one window I could see out of into the front yard and began barking in my deepest, most threatening voice. Adam's house was very confusing because there were security gates everywhere. So many doors and locks to unlock. It wasn't straight forward to get in and out. He had, had to do this because he had been robbed and held up at gun point so many times.

On this particular day, he came through to the lounge and shouted 'Shut up Finley! OUTSIDE!' All I was doing was trying to guard his house for him. But it turned out to be garden service and I had annoyed him by barking and now they were scared to come into the yard.

So I turned and went back to my Moms room. I didn't want to go outside with these strangers. Everyone who knows me will tell you how skittish I can be. I am naturally a very wary dog and people have to earn my trust. Once they have done that, I will protect them with my life. But I don't trust people for the most part and I have realized in my short time, most of them have a hidden agenda.

Besides I felt safe in my Moms room because her smell was there and all her belongings. She had also said to Adam 'Dad, there is no need for the maid to go into my room. I have cleaned it, put fresh linen on the bed and vacuumed. The room is clean, and the maid has a lot of work to do as it is.'

To be honest, I felt quite scared. The house and garden was filling up with people I didn't know. The servant had brought her baby to work on her back. There were smells I was picking up that were sending off warning bells in my head. I felt threatened without really knowing where the threat was coming from.

The garden had around ten people wandering around with different noisy machines, and it was all a bit much for me. My nerves were shot. I was hungry, unsure of where to go next, missing my Mom, and felt incredibly alone. I would just stay in her room. It was the safest place. Or so I thought!

Adam found me in the bedroom and shouted his usual 'OUTSIDE! Footsack' so I jumped down from the bed and ran for the outside door. As I got to the lounge and the garden door was in sight, blocking my way wanting to talk to 'the boss' were two garden workers.

I was too scared to run past them. So I ran back into my Moms room with Adam chasing me and screaming 'You fucking disobedient dog. OUTSIDE!' So I ran to get out my Moms room and the passage way was blocked by the servant with the baby on her back and who was now lifting carpets to sweep.

In my frantic mind, I remembered the kitchen door. I would go out that way. It was closed. I had nowhere to escape.

I found myself running in circles. My fear was so extreme, I couldn't think straight. That's when Adam went and fetched his sjambok. He thought I was just being 'full of shit' and would teach me a lesson that when he spoke, I listened. I needed discipline. He was too blind to see my fear and notice how terrified and trapped I was. I ran back to the safety of my Moms room and hid in the corner next to the side table making myself as small as possible. Adam followed me and brought the whip down on my back. I have never felt pain like that in my life. I was howling from the pain, and down it came again, even harder than the first time. I was yelping and showing my teeth at the same time. I wanted nothing more than to sink my teeth into him, but I knew he would probably kill me.

'You growling at me and baring your teeth? Well you won't be when I am finished with you!' and he was right, he broke me that day. That sjambok rained down on me several times. In the end I was weeing and pooing everywhere, and using his feet along with the sjambok, he got me outside telling the gardeners 'if this fucking dog gives you a hard time, you use this sjambok!' Just as he was leaving he shouted to the servant 'Clean up that fucking dogs mess!' and off he went to work.

I couldn't move. My body and spirit were broken. One of the gardeners left the side gate open, so I ran through that and into the garage. There I found a spot behind a couple of boxes to lie down. I was in excruciating pain. The pain from the whippings had gone deep into my soul, my ribs felt broken from the kicking and my healed broken leg was very sore where he had kicked me.

My Mom had said 'call me Finley if you need me' She always sensed when something was wrong with me, would she sense this? Would she come home now and protect me? With what little energy I had left, I tried calling her mentally.

That evening before Adam came home, I ran out the garage and found a hiding place in the front of the garden because I knew Adam would find me in the garage. The electric gate opened and he drove his car into the garage. I stayed put. I was so tempted to slip back into the garage, but not at the risk of another beating.

The garage door closed and that was me, stuck in the front garden with no way out and on my own in a hidden spot. He realized at some point that I wasn't in the house. I could hear him outside 'FINLEY! Come here! FINLEY' I never moved a muscle. Later that same night he came out drunk and it was more 'FINLEY! Fucking dog. FINLEY' and he eventually gave up and passed out I suspect.

That night outside in the front garden was horrible. My body was wracked in pain, and there was so much evil in the air. I was too scared to breathe in case I was heard. People were walking the streets prowling for houses to break into. I saw a few loose hanging arms, holding guns. Then a few Police patrol cars whizzed by. There were shots fired that night. This was an awful place. I longed to be back home in England on our farm.

I spent what energy I had that night, trying my best to call my Mom in my mind. Eventually I managed to fall asleep in my hiding place.

Next morning was Thursday. I overheard a conversation that he was going to Esme this day for a few days. Then my Mom phoned. I heard him saying 'Forget about that bloody dog and concentrate on your fucking job! Don't phone me again about this dog. I am busy man, and don't have time for your pettiness. Do your job! Your dog is fine!'

So she had phoned to check up on me. I had just missed the previous calls. I had another whole day and night to get through and to hide. It was now three days since I had eaten. I had drunk the last of the water from the bird bath yesterday. My body was in more pain today, than yesterday.

I was finding it difficult to breathe, and my leg was very sore. It was aching so much I was struggling to walk on it. Again the phone rang 'What the hell is wrong with you Danny? Your bloody dog is fine. You need to stop this bullshit my girl. You have a job to think of. If you keep phoning me about Finley, how the hell are you concentrating at work? I am leaving shortly. Yes of course he has eaten. I don't know where he is, outside I suppose. You can sense something is wrong? You just bloody paranoid about this dog. He is fine! I will make sure he is fed and watered before I leave OK? Now relax and do your bloody job. I don't have the time for this conversation'

Thank God, my Mother was getting my message. She knew something was wrong. I just had to get through today, tonight, and tomorrow and my 5 minutes was up. I decided I had to sneak into the garage when he was reversing out so that I was safely locked away. I didn't want to spend another night outside alone.

With my plan set, Adam came outside again looking for me 'FINLEY? FINLEY?' over and over he called me and I stayed hidden. He searched that garden flat and he didn't find me. I had found a good hiding place and if I didn't move or breathe I could and did go unnoticed. Even though at one point I thought he was staring right at me, he didn't see me.

Eventually he gave up and under his breath he said 'Well, suit yourself. Hopefully you have fucking run away and my daughter can concentrate on her bloody job!' He took his bags to his car, climbed inside, started the engine, and began to reverse. I quickly slipped into the garage, just before the electric garage door had shut completely.

I heard him drive off and I was in the dark, and the safety of the garage, alone. It was a big double garage, so I had plenty of space, but I was sore, terrified, thirsty and incredibly hungry. I was weary. I remember I had no energy at all. I was not seeing properly, my eye sight seemed to be affected and I was very weak.

I must have fallen into a deep sleep and not even realized the garage door was opening. I woke up startled and terrified. This woman climbed out of the car and I hobbled to hide myself in the corner. I was shaking like a leaf, growling and threatening her. 'Oh my God! Finley! It's me. Finely? What the hell has happened to you?' she was crying and made her way over to me.

All my senses were out of sync. I honestly didn't know who this woman was and I was terrified. So I kept up the growl and baring of my teeth. I couldn't walk properly, so kept stumbling. 'Finny Foo, it's me.' She sobbed. I realized then with the 'Finny Foo' it was my Mom. I cowered my way over and dropped at her feet.

I remember she cried and cried and cried. She opened the house, and carried me into the bedroom. It was hours later, after she had calmed me down, checked me over, had fed me and given me water that I began to feel just a little like my old self.

That is when she allowed her own emotions to come to the fall. Sadly, I could not tell her exactly what had happened to me. But we were very in tune with each other and always have been. While she was on the phone to my Nan, telling her the sate she had found me in, alone in a garage that she began putting the pieces of the puzzle together.

She wasn't entirely correct on her story, because how could she know for sure? But she was smart enough to get the gist of it and she knew beyond a shadow of doubt, that the sjambok had been used and she was right. She suspected I had hurt my leg while trying to run. No, it was hurt because Adam kicked me and he just managed to get my still sensitive, once broken, leg.

But it doesn't matter. She will never know the full story of what took place, but she knew enough to get us out of there.

She told my Nan 'Mom I have to go. I knew something was wrong. I couldn't concentrate at work. I was only meant to come home tomorrow night. I spoke to my boss, made up some bullshit and hit the road. I have taken tomorrow as leave. Christ I have only been at this job for three days and all this has happened. I knew I couldn't rely on Adam. I will never, so long as I breathe air into my lungs, forgive him for what he did to Finley.'

When my Nan asked her what she was going to do next? She said she would phone Harper. By all accounts Harper and her ex-husband Jason, owned two very large newly built houses that had been standing empty for a couple of years due to the economic climate in South Africa. She was going to beg Harper to help us. If that didn't work, she would find a hotel that would take us in.

Whatever was going to happen, we were leaving Adam and Witbank for good. That night with the love of my Mom, I began to come right. My body was still very sore, but my soul was feeling safe for the first time in days. She never phoned her Dad that night and he never phoned her either. She said to me 'If I never hear from that man again, it will be too soon. I don't want to speak to him.'

The following morning after we had both had a good solid rest she put her plan into action. She telephoned Harper, who agreed to speak to her ex and get back to my mom on whether they could help. Harper did say, if Jason said no, then we are to come to her house and she will make a plan regarding her cats and business. My Mom was not to worry, and she must start packing and getting our stuff together, because come what may, we had a safe place to lay our heads.

Mom thanked her very much and began packing all our stuff up again. It was later that morning that her Dad phoned. He had phoned her office and found out she had taken a day's leave and was in fact at his house. 'What the hell did you take a day's leave for? You have just started this job and you being irresponsible already! That is not the blood that runs through your veins. We don't shirk responsibilities.' He yelled at her.

'I cannot believe you have the gall to phone me after what you have done to Finley. Don't you dare, speak to me about responsibilities. What you have done to Finley is criminal and by rights I should lay a charge of assault against you. I trusted you. I begged you. I believed, that just this once, you would be someone I could rely on to do the honourable thing. All you had to do, was leave him alone, fill a bowl up with food and water and be kind. You have failed miserably and I will never, ever forgive you for what you have done.

Finley cannot tell me, but I am not stupid. I have a very deep connection with this dog and I know for a fact, you used that sjambok on him and you have hurt him. Correction, you have broken him! You are a bastard. I found him cowering in abstract pain in the garage all alone. You have hurt his broken leg as well. You are a cruel man and one I am so ashamed of. I have nothing further to say to you.' She replied through her sobbing.

'I want you and that dog out of my fucking house! You do not speak to me in that tone of voice and expect to get away with it. I am your Father and I demand respect from you. Get out my fucking house now! I want my keys back as well. You leave those keys at my pub with Bill, and I never want to hear from you again.' He shouted.

Mom was shaking so much. She tried to make a cup of tea to calm down and was spilling the water as she poured it from the kettle. My Mom always answered the phone on loud speaker unless she was in public, and hearing Adam's voice, made me start trembling too. I had to keep correcting myself. When I heard his voice, I wanted to run and hide. It was terrifying for me.

We both sat there shaking uncontrollably for ages before she could pour water in her mug, drink her tea, and we both calmed down to a quiet panic. She worked very quickly. Pulling stuff out the cupboard and just throwing it into black plastic bags and shoving what she could into suitcases. I could sense she too, was terrified, he would get in his car and drive the one and a half hours back before we had time to leave.

That's when Harper phoned 'Hi chick. I have spoken to Jason. You and Finley can stay in the cottage of the one house in Alphen Park. Chick I am sorry, but he wants R2500 (£118) a month for you to stay there. When you ready, just come through to me, and I will give you all the keys you need. I, in the meantime, am going to find what old furniture I can, and do what I can to make it comfortable for you. I am really sorry Chick. I hope you and Finley are OK. Let me know once you on the road so I know how much time I have left to get everything done.'

'Thank you Harper. I don't care if it's a tent in the garden. As long as we have somewhere to lay our head, I am only too grateful. I have two months to get through before relocating to Durban. I am just packing things up here quickly. I am so scared Adam decides to drive home. Let me go, and again, thank you for helping us out. I really do appreciate it. I will give you the rent when I see you later' she replied.

I think we both breathed an enormous sigh of relief. I have not seen my mom so shaken up ever. Although she had managed to drink her tea without spilling it, her hands were still shaking and I could sense she was not thinking clearly. I felt sorry for her. This was a tough time we were both going through, but I must be honest, I was thanking Anubis most sincerely for opening another door for us and for the fact that I would never have to see Adam again.

Once the car was packed, she ran through the house to check she hadn't forgotten anything, washed her cup, dried it and packed it away. Checked all the doors were locked and opened the boot for me to jump into. She had put the car seats down to create more space. If I thought the car was loaded when I jumped in, I was in for a surprise.

'Fin, I am going to stop at Pep Stores. I need to buy a few bits and pieces. We also need to get you more food and I need toiletries. I won't be long. Look after the car for me. I'll be 5 minutes' and with that, I was in the parking lot again, guarding our stuff until she returned.

I saw her walking back to the car and I remember thinking 'You have got to be kidding me! Where the hell are you planning on putting all that stuff?' she opened the boot and said 'Sorry Finny Foo, but these are necessities for our new move. With that she shoved two large packets, and I mean large, into the boot, taking up more of the little bit of space I had left.

She could have done this shopping in Benoni, but she knew where Pep Store was in Witbank and it was easier for her. She was tired, stressed and when we got to where we were going, she didn't want to have to go out again. Pep she explained to me is a very cheap store. It's a shop for people who are living on a shoe string budget and below the bread line.

Everything you buy there is of poor quality, but it works and serves its purpose. She told me, she had bought, a fitted sheet, a duvet cover, pillows, a blanket, washing up liquid, towels, one knife, one fork, one teaspoon, one table spoon, one cutting knife, one mug, one plate, toilet paper, soap, shampoo, two small rugs, a bucket, an ashtray, kitchen cloths, dish towels and a dustbin.

The rugs she explained were to make the cottage we were moving into, feel just a little bit like home. It was to bring some warmth. The other packet, had a bottle of Whisky, my food, tea, coffee, long life milk, bread, butter, Bovril, sugar, a packet of chocolate biscuits, two minute noodles and two cheap pots.

I remember when she closed the boot, my tail had no place to go. Although I have a fairly short tail compared to other dogs, I have lots of wispy hair on it which makes it look long. She kept curling it up and placing it next to me to shut the boot and it would naturally uncurl and she couldn't close the boot without catching my hair. In the end she said to me 'Finley, hold onto this will you! I have to get this door closed and your tail is in the way. Once I have closed it, you can relax. It's only for one hour Finny Foo.' With that, she put my tail in my mouth and I held onto it until the boot was slammed shut.

This was going to be one bloody hot, nightmare hour. I quite literally, had no way of lying down. I did however end up lying scrunched on the packets and she had opened the back window so I at least had the hot air blowing in. I remember it was a stinking hot day again. The temperatures most days were in the high 30's and I assume it was no less on that day. I was melting in the boot.

But we were both so happy. I was cramped up, my body still sore and my leg still a bit achy, but the energy between us was good. She played Fleetwood Mac and sang, and every now and then, she would talk to me through the review mirror and I would bark and wag my tail showing her I am just fine. We often communicated when in the car, through the review mirror.

Being cramped was a very small hardship to go through, because I knew it was all over. Even though I was sweating out last night's water, I knew we were going somewhere we could and would both heal. So all the discomfort would be worth it.

Chapter 5

We finally arrived at Harper who gave Mom a big bunch of keys and a map on how to get to the house. She said to Mom 'Chick, I have done what I can furniture wise in the short time I have had to prepare. It's not very nice, but it's at least something. If I can help in any other way, please just let me know.' And Mom handed Harper R2500.

We didn't hang around. Thankfully Mom was very mindful of the fact I was dying from heat stroke and a lack of boot space. My tongue was hanging out the side of my mouth, and I was beginning to lose my sense of humour and optimism.

Off we drove again, armed with a big bunch of keys, a map, and instructions on which key fits which door. We drove through a gated security check where they took my Moms details and phoned Harper to confirm that we were indeed allowed to drive onto this gated community and have access to the house. Once that was all established, with a few left and right turns, we had arrived at what would be our home for the next six weeks.

Mom managed to open the electric garage. Once in, she climbed out the car 'Finley, give me a few minutes will you. I have to find a red button. Harper says there is a red button in this garage that I press to close the garage door. For some reason the remote will only open the garage doors' With that she was searching all over that double garage. I could hear her 'where the fuck is this bloody red button?' She was also pouring with sweat and we had both reached the end of our tether.

Twenty minutes later and with sweat dripping off my eyelashes and the salt stinging my eyes, I heard her on the phone 'Harper, where in God's name is this fucking red button? I have searched this garage flat and there is nothing.'

'Danny if you look above your head towards the light, on the one side, I can't remember which side, is a little red button, push that chick' said Harper laughing her head off.

'You have got to be kidding me! Why didn't you tell me that is where it is? Finley has melted into a wet rug, and I am ready to explode from frustration.' Replied my Mom. With that she pushed the elusive red button and praise Anubis the garage door closed. I could finally get out of this bloody small boot.

Not realizing she was parked on a slope, she opened the boot and I quite literally, fell out! Mom peeled into laughter. She was laughing so much, she was crying. 'Oh Finley, I am sorry. I didn't realise you were that close to the boot door.' She spurted out through peals of laughter. Seriously? She didn't know how tight it was in the boot? I was not impressed. I hit that ground with a thud. I gave her my incredulous look that had her peel into fresh laughter. I did not see anything funny in that. I was really quite indignant.

'Oh common Fin. Don't be angry, I didn't know the slope was that steep and I certainly didn't know you were that close to the boot door. Sorry Foo. Common, we have to find our home and get these packets to where ever it is we staying. Let's go and investigate. I know there is a swimming pool here.' She said. All I heard was, swimming pool. That put a wag in my tail.

She grabbed the big bunch of keys and off we went. Harper had very cleverly colour coded all the keys with nail varnish and given a card with each colour and which door it belonged to. So the pink blob of nail varnish was the garage door leading to the house. The purple blob of nail varnish, was for the door leading to the landing of the main house. The blue blob of nail varnish, was for the door leading off the landing onto an iron staircase which led outside to the ground level and where we would be staying. The red blob of nail varnish, was for our front door.

So with all the blobs sorted out and keys in hand, we made our way into the unknown. Door one, open, door two, open, door three open. That is where it ended for me. There was no way I was going down those iron stairs. Nope! I refuse! 'Common Finley! You go up and down stairs all the time in England. They no different to Nana's steps that you and Gordie chase up and down on. Common boy.' begged my Mom.

Nope! I was not going down those stairs. They certainly were not the same as my Nana's steps. They looked very scary to me. They were narrow, and twisted in an S bend. I could also see through them to the floor and having just fallen out the boot of the car, I was not going to risk falling through one of these gaps. I will stay here I told her.

'Finley, for God sake! Common, I can't carry you. You too heavy and we will both fall down these stairs. Please Finley.' She begged. Nope! I absolutely refused. I am not moving one muscle towards those perilous steps. I had, had enough. No way. So I backed up completely and lay on the other side of the landing. Forget it. I am not going down those stairs. 'Jeepers you a pain in the bum Finley. OK, let me unload the car and I will try and carry you down' she muttered. So she was backwards and forwards with suitcases, black plastic bags, shopping bags, a tennis racket and whatever else had taken up all my space. I just lay there watching her.

From the bottom and after the last load had been taken down the stairs, she yelled up at me 'Finley, I am going for a swim, common boy, you need to cool down too. Common Fin, you can do the stairs, I know you can. Common boy' Nope! She couldn't tempt me with a BBQ lamb chop, so a swimming pool was not going to do it.

'For crying out loud Finley, if we both end up dead at the bottom of these stairs, it will all be your fault' she said while walking up the stairs for the umpteenth time to fetch me. I remember thinking, what? Dead? Falling? You wasting your time Mom, I am digging my paws in. I refuse to go down that thing.

In the end she caught me, picked me up 'Finley, lie still will you. These are dangerous steps. I nearly fell taking the cases down. They narrow and not easy. Don't make it any worse for me by struggling. You bloody heavy and this is not going to be easy. Lie still!' I did as she asked, wagged my tail and down we went. One dangerous step at a time.

Finally we reached the bottom. My Mom put me down, and flopped onto the concrete ground herself to catch her breath. The sweat was pouring from her face. Her T shirt was drenched from sweat, her hair all wet, stringy and scrunched up in an elastic band, her arm muscles were aching and she was exhausted.

'Happy now?' she asked in that agitated tone she would use sometimes with me. Yes! Wagging my tail. I was now happy. Now where was that pool you were talking about? She opened the last door with the red blob on the key, literally, dragged all the stuff into the cottage, left it all in the front room, took her clothes off down to her bra and panties and her and I walked to the swimming pool.

She dove in without even feeling the temperature of the water. I dove in straight after her. She was laughing, I was wagging my tail under the water. Oh I remember the joy. How good that water felt. How happy we were. Both of us had forgotten about the dreaded stairs, our road trip, the falling out the boot, the lost red button in the garage, and most importantly, the trauma we went through with Owen and then Adam.

We swam and swam. It was amazing. I would climb out the pool, run around barking, and jump back in. Chew at the water while swimming, out again, run around the pool and dive back in. Mom then disappeared leaving me to carry on swimming and returned with her fancy Pep Store glass, filled with whisky and water along with her packet of ciggies and ashtray. She sat on the top step of the swimming pool and by that stage, I was lying on her towel and we both just sat there in silence having a good look at our surroundings and taking it all in.

This was truly a beautiful home. The swimming pool was accessed directly from the main house with its large glass doors and nothing to obstruct the magnificent view. It seemed the whole house was made of window and chrome. Every room looked out on this area. Mom called me and said 'Fin come have a look inside here' she was peering through the glass doors into the massive lounge and open plan kitchen. I pushed my snout up against the glass and looking inside, she was right, it was lovely.

We had come to the pool via a side gate. The whole pool area was marble laid. Looking ahead were well manicured lawns that led to the water's edge. A large lake lay in front of us. The only way to access it, was if you were lucky enough to own one of these very expensive houses whose lawns extended down to the water. Or you were a really good swimmer and brave enough to swim the mile across from the other side.

On the lake people were on paddle boards. Others had canoes and others were just swimming for exercise. There were loads of Hadada birds in the garden. They black and greyish and have a huge bill. These are quite large birds, they look something like a Stalk. They make the strangest sound 'haa-haa-haa-de-dah'

I was a bit weary of them at first. But I soon got comfortable and decided to see how well they could fly when chased. No matter how many times I chased them, they would hover up above me, wait for me to move on, and just come back down again. They really had a bad attitude. Almost a mocking one of 'catch me if you can'

After sitting at the pool for what seemed like ages, Mom said 'Thank you god. Thank you for helping us to move in here. It's so beautiful and so good for the soul. I really am so grateful.'' I agreed with her so I thanked Anubis too. This place was great. Once the sun had set on the water, Mom said 'Common Fin, lets unpack our stuff and sort dinner out.' With that we left the pool area and walked the short distance back to our cottage next to the dreaded stairs.

The cottage was very small. As you opened the door there was probably a two meter passage way with three doors coming off it. To the right was the shower and toilet. To the left, was the lounge come dining room, come kitchen. Straight ahead was a small bedroom. The lounge was very small. You could have a small two seater sofa in there, maybe a chair or two, a book case perhaps, a plant, but not much more than that or you would have no space to stand and cook.

The kitchen part of that lounge was a long wall to wall counter, with a few built in cupboards at the top and bottom. A small space underneath for a washing machine perhaps and a small space at the end for an oven. Not sure where you would stand your fridge. Either way it was very small and although this was meant to be a 'granny flat' who ever moved in here permanently would find it difficult with the floor space.

The bedroom had built in wardrobes and your double bed slotted between the floor to ceiling wardrobes. The wardrobes were a bit awkward because the one narrow cupboard had hanging space, but not much at all. The other long cupboard on the other side of the bed had shelving and right at the top, you could perhaps store stuff. This was not a cupboard for someone like Chichi's Mother, who flew to Dubai to do her shopping!

Once the bed was in, there was very little room to move around and also it had one very small window right at the top of the one wall which meant it was very dark. No sun light reached that room so you would always need the light on even on the sunniest day. Also it was very stuffy, so I didn't sleep in there. I preferred to sleep in the lounge area.

In the lounge, Harper had left us an old, very worn out double seater, caramel coloured leather sofa. A deck chair. Another whitish leather type single arm chair. A narrow wooden, lounge cabinet type table with two draws and a little side table.

In the kitchen Harper had left us a two plate stove, two cups, some knives and forks, and a couple of plates. I was beginning to realise why Mom had stopped and bought the few little pretties she had. She rearranged the few small pieces of furniture, put her one rug on the lounge floor and the other in the bathroom.

On that narrow wooden dresser type table in the lounge, she put a photo album of her Nana and Grandad which my Nan had made for her, and next to that, the photo she has had next to her bed since I have known her. A photo of her as a baby with her Nana who she always said she loved very dearly.

She made her bed with her new linen and unpacked the rest of the items she had bought putting them in the kitchen area. So hanging a dish towel, putting a dishcloth on the sink along with the washing up liquid. She put the bin out, put her ashtray on the little side table next to the sofa. Put the soap and shampoo in the shower area, along with tooth brush, toothpaste and hair brush. Hung up her two towels which she said were no bigger than the dish towels she had bought but they would serve their purpose. Unpacked all her clothes and only realized then, she had no hangers! After that, we were pretty much done.

My Snoozzee bed was put in the lounge.

'Finley I know you probably not going to sleep on this, and you probably don't like where I have put it, so you can move it or sleep on the sofa.' She said. She was right, I didn't like my bed being behind the sofa in the little kitchen part. So I dragged it into the lounge where I had a view outside from the windows. Once I had finished dragging it to where I wanted it, she straightened it all out for me and we stood back to look at our new home. It was small, it was sparse, but it was ours. No one was going to interfere with us, and we had very little to be scared of in here.

Yes there were always house break in's and the crime was bad, but for some reason, we felt safe here tucked under the horrid staircase. That first night, to be honest, I think we were both so tired, a bomb could have gone off and we would not have heard it.

Next morning was Saturday. Mom got up early, opened up the front door so I could go into the yard and do my business while she made a cup of tea. She had taken one item that didn't belong to her from Adam's house and it was an old stainless steel camping kettle which she still has today. Adam was going to throw it away because he had no use for it. So she decided to take it when we left.

I was still wondering around the garden, when I saw her come through the side gate with her tea and smokes. She sat on the veranda looking out at the lake and I noticed for the first time in ages, she was at peace. Her energy had changed. This was more like the Mother I knew. I came and lay next to her and we both just sat in silence. No barking from me, and no phone calls on loud speaker. At 06h00 in the morning, it is so quiet and peaceful.

'Fin, we going to have to go and do some shopping today. We don't have a fridge, so I am going to buy a cooler box and ice. I need to be able to keep just a few things like milk fresh. I also need hangers for my clothes, and I need to buy a bucket I can wash my clothes in along with pegs.' She said. 'Don't worry, you can come with in the car' she added on seeing my face drop at the thought of being left alone. I wagged my tail and fell asleep while she finished her tea.

After that, she picked up my poos from the lawn and we both made our way back to the cottage. Soon it would be breakfast time and Mom always made both of us toast with Bovril and along with her second cup of tea, she would make one for me with an extra teaspoon of sugar for my sweet tooth and put it in my bowl'

'Fin, I am going to have a shower, get dressed and then we going shopping OK?' she said as she left the lounge. I wagged my tail but she didn't see. Next minute I heard her squealing 'Oh shit! There is no hot water!' she was sure there must be a power switch to turn the water on. So together we searched that little cottage and found nothing. She was phoning Harper.

'Hi girl, sorry to be a pain, but where do I switch the hot water on? I have just climbed into the shower and its only cold water and its bloody cold water!' Harper was laughing and said 'Danny, I am sorry, I forgot to tell you, there is no hot water in the cottage yet. We still have to sort that out. I am really sorry girl. If you want a hot bath or shower you will have to come to my house.' Which really wasn't convenient because Harper lived across town from us.

With that, my Mom jumped into the shower all I heard were high pitched sounds. Moans and gasps coming from the bathroom. She came out shivering, teeth chattering and clutching a small towel to dry herself. It did make me smile. It was so funny to watch her hopping around and trying to warm herself up and dry herself with these small towels which she said didn't absorb the water. All they did was move the water from one part of the body to the other.

She could see my amused expression and simply said 'Don't laugh Finley! That was bloody cold. We moving out of summer and into winter and Johannesburg gets damn cold in winter. I hope we at Lala before the real cold sets in. Cold showers like this will be the death of me'

Lala, was Moms other Granny. She was my Gramps mother and I had only ever heard wonderful things about her. We would be staying with Lala when we moved to Durban. Mom finally warmed up, got dressed, picked up the car keys and said 'Common Fin lets go' It was then I realized that to get to the car, I had to climb the dreaded staircase.

My Mother didn't even look back. 'Finley, I refuse to carry you up these stairs, so you either climb up the damn stairs, or you can wait at home for me. Your choice boy. If I get to the top and you not with me, you can stay.' And up she went. I stood at the bottom watching her adamant not to climb the stairs.

From the top she said 'You coming or staying here Finley?' She waited around for a while and said 'So be it. I will be 5 minutes Fin.' and off she walked leaving me behind. I heard the car drive out, the electric garage shut and was guttered she hadn't carried me up the stairs and now I was all alone and wouldn't get to see the parking lot and keep the car safe.

I vowed that would be the last time she left me behind. I had to conquer these stairs if it was the last thing I did. So while she was away, I began with one step at a time. I would get to step five, and run back down again. I was determined to get up these stairs but they really were very scary for me. In the end and minutes before I heard the garage door opening, I made it to the top. I had done it!

I had conquered my fear. Boy was Mom surprised when she used the key with the pink blob on and found me on the landing inside the entrance to the main house. 'Finley! You did it!' she said laughing while hugging and kissing me. 'Well done my precious child. I knew you could do it. Well done Finny Foo. That is an amazing accomplishment. I am so proud of you.' She was saying while clapping her hands in praise.

I was beaming with pride. My whole body was wagging. I had done it. I had managed to climb all the way up and now all I had to do, was get down again. But I wasn't going to show her I was terrified. She didn't know I had only climbed up and not down yet. But I was going to do this if it killed me. Down mom went with all her packets and a big cooler box. I quite literally took one step every three minutes, but I got down on my own to another big round of applause from my Mom.

Once she opened her packets a whole load of treats came out for me. One of which was a fantastic fresh marrow bone. So I took that from her, and lay outside chewing and licking my delicious bone, while she unpacked. She had bought all the goodies she said she needed and the surprise was a little CD player. I was chewing my bone and out the cottage came the sound of Neil Diamond.

We love Neil Diamond and I always dance to Holly Holy with my Mom by standing on my back legs and she holds my paws. It's our song. It was wonderful to hear music in the house and her singing again. Mom was faffing around sweeping and doing her washing outside in a bucket and I was enjoying my bone.

She would fill the bucket up with cold water from the outside tap, put some soap powder in, and wash her clothes by hand. Then chuck the soapy water down the drain, fill the bucket up again, and rinse her clothes. Now that she had hangers, she could hang her washing on hangers outside to dry. She didn't have an iron, so she tried really hard to make sure she had shaken the creases out as best she could.

That first Saturday in the cottage was the first of many lovely days. It was on that day when Mom had finished the washing and I had pretty much finished my bone that we went for our usual swim. Mom got a big fright because she was lying on her towel when around the corner out of nowhere came this man.

She was so startled and thankfully this time wearing a costume. He said 'I am sorry Miss. My name is Miles and I work for Harper and Jason. I look after their properties. I do the gardening, clean the pools, keep the houses safe and live in the cottage next door on the property of other empty house. I didn't mean to frighten you.'

'Phew Miles, you nearly gave me a heart attack! My name is Danny and it's a pleasure to meet you. This is Finley.' Mom replied while shaking Miles's hand. She was struggling to get over the fact that I never barked or attacked Miles. I could read her whirling thoughts. Truth is, I didn't get a bad smell from him and in fact I liked him very much. So I didn't really see the need for any fuss.

Miles would become my friend and companion during the days when Mom was at work and we would have loads of fun together. 'I wanted to give you my phone number Miss Danny. Just in case you ever need me for anything.' Miles said and so they exchanged mobile numbers and my Mom was very thankful to him. With that, he explained he just needed to put some chemicals in the pool to keep the water nice and blue for her and he would be off and leave her in peace.

Later she phoned Harper and was told Miles had worked for them for fifteen years and was their most trusted and reliable employee. He by all accounts had keys to every nook and cranny of both empty properties. My Mom wasn't entirely happy that he had a key to our cottage. So Harper said she would remove the key and rightly so, no one should have a key to my Moms cottage. It was our private space and we were paying rent for that. That made Mom feel a lot safer.

She didn't even want Jason to have a key and warned Harper to please tell Jason that he must not go in the cottage without her being there because I bite and am very protective of my home. Well, she wasn't lying. I don't care who it is and to be honest, I don't even care if you have been in my home before. If anyone comes to my front door, I am going to go crazy. It is my duty to protect my Mom and our belongings. Plus I am especially edgy when I am left alone.

To be honest, that first weekend went by so quickly and it was back to work for Mom on the Monday. She used to leave me outside when she went to work. I didn't mind. She always brought my bed out and put it under the shelter of the staircase where it was cool and even if it rained, it would always stay dry. I had a huge bucket filled with water along with a bowl full of dry biscuits, which as you know, I hate, but mom called it emergency food.

So at least if she was ever later or held up, I would not go hungry like I had done at Adam. Plus I had Miles who I would follow around and help with the digging up of the garden and the cleaning of the swimming pool. My days were full. As mom would leave for work, Miles would appear 'Hello Finley. Today, I have to clear the leaves at the water's edge. The boss also wants me to cut down a tree, and I need to plant some vegetables next door at the other house. Common lets go.'

My days were planned. It was very exciting for me. I would drag Miles's garden broom around and hide it for fun. I especially loved digging where he had his spade to create furrows to plant his seeds. The best was when he was cutting trees or pruning them, branches would fall and I would drag those to our cottage door to chew on later.

Then we always had time for a swim and Miles would share his food with me at lunch time. So I got to eat lots of delicious meat and stuff called Mealie Meal. My Mom could never understand why I was not hungry at dinner time until Miles explained that he cooks for both of us at lunch time and he likes to share his meal with me.

Mom would phone Miles every day to check things were OK and that I was behaving myself and there was no drama unfolding that she needed to be aware of. The answers were always the same 'Hello Miss Danny. Finley is fine, he is very good. Nothing to worry about.'

All this allowed my Mom to finally concentrate on her very big new job. A couple of weeks into this she came home one night and said 'Finely I have to go to Durban on a business trip for five days. I obviously cannot leave you here. I have spoken to my boss and he has said I am to drop you at his house. He has three other dogs and he will take care of you for the days I am away.'

Dammit man. I hated being left with strangers and why I couldn't just stay with Miles, I don't know. Something about it not being safe. Anything could happen to Miles and after Adam's experience she was taking no chances. She would feel safer leaving me with doggie lovers and people who saw their dogs as family members and not just outdoor killing machines.

I guess I understood. The last thing I needed or wanted, was a repeat of what I had gone through with Adam and if anything happened to Miles, I would be left in that exact position if not worse. So I wagged my tail while barking and she knew, I was fine with going to her boss's house.

Next day, she packed my Snoozzee, grabbed my food bowl, her small travel bag, locked the house up and said 'Let's go Fin. You will see Miles in a few days' I ran up the stairs and was at the top in seconds. I was fast up those stairs and very chuffed when she started laughing.

We drove through to my Moms boss and I was really very pleased when I got there. They were really nice people and I liked my Moms boss, his wife and their dogs, immediately. I knew I was going to have a great time here. They had a Basset with the longest ears I had ever seen. A tan Labrador and a Jack Russel like Gordie. They were happy dogs and they welcomed me in.

Mom said goodbye 'Finley, please be a good boy. No biting. No fighting. Do not climb on the sofa unless you are invited to do so. Be nice to the other dogs. Remember you are the guest. Not them! I will be 5 minutes and I will come and pick you up again. I love you Finny Foo.' She gave me a few hooter kisses and off she drove to the airport.

I was fine. She really can sometimes panic for nothing. I had a great time at her boss's house. I was allowed on the sofa, on the beds, on the outdoor furniture, in the swimming pool, and in all, it was a holiday for me. Her boss fed us all fantastic food. My bowl was always full of water and I got on famously with my new friends.

To be honest, the next time I looked up, was when my Moms car pulled up and I heard her voice. I was so happy to see her face. Although I had really enjoyed my time with her boss, I loved my Mom so much and I was always happy to see her and know we were going to be together again. I was wagging my body and barking seeing her at the gate.

Her boss said to her 'Danny, Finley was amazing. He is one of, if not thee, smartest dog I have known. He is an absolute delight and it was a pleasure looking after him. We all fell in love with him. If you ever need a home for him or you ever need somewhere to leave him, he is welcome back here anytime.'

To which my Mom replied laughing 'Thank you Adrian. Yes Finley is an incredible boy. Too bloody clever for his own good! I can see he has had the best time and thank you most sincerely for looking after him as well as you did. Thank you for your kind offer of looking after Finley if I ever need somewhere to leave him'

She never did comment on him wanting to give me a home. He knew and I knew, that would never happen. As much as I liked Adrian and his family, they were not my Mom and I would never leave her side. We were destined to make old bones together.

Finally we were on our way back to the cottage and Mom was telling me all about her trip. 'Gee Finley, the trip was so interesting. I went with two blokes from the UK. One of which I know quite well. He used to be a client of mine when I worked in Groupages back in England. I have my work cut out for me. This is a huge project and responsibility that has been given to me and one that is going to be tough to get up and running.

It was bloody hot in Durban. Humid, sticky, and sweaty, but it was lovely to be back. You won't believe who I saw, Steve!' My ears picked up, Steve? Wow! How did that happen I was asking her in the review mirror.

'Steve is in South Africa for a little holiday. You know Steve. From Mauritius, instead of flying back to England, he decided to stay on a few more weeks in Durban and spend time with is old friends. Actually Fin, he had some very bad news. He has been diagnosed with a serious heart condition and will need an operation within the next few months. I am very concerned for him. He has to go for more tests on his return and he will give me the details of what they find.

He told me he is unsure of whether to have his op done in the UK or in South Africa. You won't know Fin, but South Africa pioneered heart transplants. They had a man called Doctor Chris Barnard. He was a South African Cardiac Surgeon who performed the world's first highly publicized heart transplant and the first one in which the patient regained consciousness. It put South Africa on the map and from there the medical side of things just grew and grew. So Steve is considering having his op done in Durban.

Personally I am not sure that is such a good idea, but it's his choice. I told him he is under a really good Surgeon at St Thomas hospital in England and that the grass was not always greener on the other side. Whatever he decides he will let us know once he returns.

Other than that? To be honest Fin, it was all office work, and meeting after meeting. I stayed in a stunning Hotel not far from the beach and had unadulterated luxury for the five days I was there. But I missed you so much. Saying that, you never called me, so I assume, you had a great time with Adrian' she finished off laughing.

It was so sad for me to hear about Steve. I really loved Steve and now he was so sick and needed this big operation. But she was also right in so far as I didn't need to call her. I had a great time while she was away. I had spent five days 'grab arsing' as my Mom calls it. That is when all us dogs chase each other, wrestle, and play fight. But she was home and we were together again and that is all that ever matters to me. No one could ever understand me or love me like she did.

After that, she rambled on about what we were going to eat for dinner, she hoped the cottage had been kept safe, and was looking forward to a swim. Loads of traffic later, we pulled up at home and it wasn't long before we were both in the pool cooling off.

It was Hadada chasing time for me, and Whisky and smoke time for Mom after our swim. We always sat together and watched the sun set on the water before starting our evening in our little cottage. It had become a daily ritual and one where we would together thank God and Anubis for all our Blessings.

After that business trip life just seemed to flow again. Mom was back at work, and I was back helping Miles out with all his garden work and sharing meals with him. My and Moms birthday was coming up in a few days' time. Mine is on the 3rd of March and Mom is on the 5th March. I would be two years old and Mom would be forty-nine.

Mom had been single and on her own now for 18 months. She had not been out on a date or met anyone. Harper had called her and said she was organizing to take Mom out with some friends and there may be one or two single blokes for dinner at a Greek Restaurant. My Mom was telling Harper 'Girl, I am really not interested. Seriously. I have no interest in meeting anyone. However, I am really looking forward to that dinner though, so thank you.'

Later, once we had eaten, Mom was sitting on the two seater sofa, it was raining outside and it was bit chilly. She had her feet up on the little side table, a glass of red wine, and I was lying on my bed. She was in a reflective mood and she began talking to me 'You know Finley, I feel as though I have sailed all the ocean tides and handled all the seasons.

I have been ruled by fear for so many years. I built my life around men, and two in particular. Owen and then Ryan. I climbed mountains for both of them and all that achieved was being brought down by a mud slide. I am not getting any younger and I am beginning to slowly see my reflection. It's been a life time since I saw myself for who and what I have become.

I have made mistakes that quite honestly, I should not have. I made my life so incredibly painful and lonely through poor choices. I am learning that less is more. Here we sit Fin, with no curtains, no fridge, no oven, no hot water, no iron, in fact no mod cons, no man, and yet I am so happy.

I feel strangely content. Would I like someone in my life? Sure I would, but this is my time. There is a healing on a great many levels that needs to take place. I cannot believe I am forty-nine in three days' time. Where have all the years gone? What have I done with this precious life that was given to me?

I feel I have to play catch up. God gave me so much and I used so little. Such misplaced trust, loyalty, and devotion. What a thief of time that has been. It has corroded my being. I thank god daily for you Finley. I always knew he would give me the strength to leave Ryan in the end and to not be afraid. We have been through so much together Fin.

You Finley, have been the most beautiful, loyal companion and friend to me. I owe you my life.'

I remember lying there, watching her, full of emotion and thinking to myself, no Mom, it is me who owes you my life. You have brought so much joy, love, laughter and happiness. You always try your hardest for me. I am so well looked after. I never want for a bone, a treat, a hot dinner, fresh water, a good brushing, or a long walk.

Whether you are ill or not. You always see to my needs first, before your own. I am the blessed one. We were meant to be together so we could heal each other. As you thank your God for bringing me into your life, I thank my God, Anubis for you arriving on that hot day in June and taking me home with you. I remember how sick I was. I had a skin disorder which meant I had no tail hair and I really felt rotten.

You did everything in your power to heal me and your love for me has been unconditional. Being overcome with emotion myself, I got up from my bed, walked over to her and rested my head on her lap. She knew, what I was saying to her. She hugged me hard, gave me hooter kisses and said 'Thank you Finny Foo'

Not long after our heart to heart, we went to bed and this time, I decided to lie with her until she fell asleep.

Once I heard she was asleep, I eased myself away from under her arm and quietly jumped off the bed and lay on the sofa in the lounge.

Mom was up early, came through to the lounge singing 'Happy birthday to you, happy birthday to you, happy birthday dear Finley, happy birthday to you. Hip hip –Horray!' and clapping her hands. Then she knelt down and gave me hooter kisses and the biggest bear hug. I could hardly breathe but it was all such fun. I was wagging my body in thanks to mom.

'Now Finny Foo. As you know, we don't have an oven, so I cannot bake a liver cake and put edible candles on it like I did last year. So, today, you and I are going to the shops, and I am going to buy cooked and already stewed oxtail from Spar! You in for some oxtail Fin?' she asked. Wow! Yes please. I love oxtail. So I started barking and doing my victory lap of running around in circles only this time, managing not to knock over the side table with the ashtray on it.

Oh this would be a great day. I always got spoilt on my birthday. True to her word, she bought a big tub of take away oxtail with mash and peas, she divided it between the two of us and we sat down to my birthday lunch. After that, I was allowed one of our chocolate biscuits. I remember having a great birthday.

Next it was Moms birthday and I tried in my way to wish her a Happy Birthday, did a victory lap for her and gave her lots of attention. She went out that night with Harper. I was happy for her, but she sensed my fear in being left alone. I still found it very scary to be on my own at night time in Africa.

'Fin, I know you feeling a bit nervous. I won't be long I promise' with that she left saying she would be home in her usual 5 minutes. She was no sooner gone and she was back. She had kept to her word and didn't leave me for too long on my own.

When she got home, she had a coffee and just told me she had a lovely meal, the company was great, and she had danced a little, but was pleased to be back home with me. She had hardly finished her sentence when it all changed.

Suddenly things turned a little scary. I could sense someone was wondering around outside by the pool area. It didn't smell like Miles and I gave Mom a stern warning. I could sense her whole body freeze. She was terrified. Although we were happy in our little cottage under the stairs, we were alone on a very big property with nowhere to run and no gun to protect us. She had to give Adam his gun back when she left. The only way out was through the side gate, into the garden and down to the water. If you made it that far under attack, the only choice you would have is to swim across the lake or negotiate your way to the next door neighbour.

If anything went wrong, there really would be no time to negotiate the stairs and use four different keys for four different doors to safety.

The corner our cottage was in, left you no place to hide. Mom was very aware of this. So on my warning with my deepest barking, she switched all the lights off. Pulled the windows closed and we sat there sweating with only the light from the moon coming into the lounge. You could hear both our hearts beating and she had asked me to please 'be quiet Finley. I need to listen'

We sat in the lounge looking out that window for ages. I was growling under my breath, but I didn't bark. Just waiting for someone to walk into our little square, but they didn't. Next thing we heard were gun shots, then police sirens, and then it all went quiet again. Whatever happened that night, it was now over. I think I remember Mom telling me a few days later that two houses further down the lake had been broken into and someone had been shot. Whether it was the robber or the victim, she never did say.

The robbers had somehow gained access to the waterfront houses using the water as their entry point, it was easy to go unnoticed because they would come in from the bottom of the garden and quietly make their way up to the main house with the weapon of their choice.

Gosh this South Africa was truly another place to live in. We didn't have all this stress back in England. Thing is most of the time, these house break ins are done in the early hours of the morning when people are in their deepest sleep.

That week, things just began to go a bit wrong. Following day Mom left for work as usual. I joined Miles on his gardening when I noticed a friend of Miles's go into our house. I went crazy. I was barking my head off and I lunged for him, so he locked himself in our house until Miles moved me away far enough for his friend to make an escape. Oh this was not good. My Mom I knew, would be very upset. Why was Miles allowing this?

That night Mom came home and was none the wiser and I had no way of telling her what had happened. The next day the same thing happened. Miles would give this man the key to our cottage, the key that was meant to have been taken away and he would go inside, lock the door and leave me outside with Miles.

Miles told me 'He is a friend. He just wants to have a shower and get some sleep. He doesn't have a home of his own and I have no more space at my cottage for him to sleep. Lots of people here are poor and sleep on the street. I am just helping him out. He won't take anything. He just wants to sleep.'

I was not happy and I did not like the smell from this man. I had to find a way of telling my Mother that someone else had a key to our home and that when she left for work, things were going on she would not be happy about. It took four days before the opportunity to tell her came.

Johannesburg was going through some terrible weather. The thunder storms could be very scary. My Mom says you have never experienced a thunder storm until you have lived in Africa. Mom would tell me it has something to do with global temperatures rising. Everyone was talking about it. The flooding was incredible. Over the past seven decades, they had become more frequent and more ferocious.

On that fourth day, Mom said to me 'Finley, I am sorry, but I am going to leave you in the cottage today. I will make a plan to come home early, but we heading for some dreadful weather. I don't want you caught outside when this thunderstorm breaks. I would feel much happier knowing you inside the cottage and away from harm's way. I promise you, I will come home early. Believe me Foo, you don't want to be outside during one of these perilous storms.'

Oh thank God for that. Now I would be able to show her what happens when she leaves for work. My plan? Well, as soon as Miles's friend opens our door, I am going to run past him at full speed and I am going to stay away from Miles too until my Mom comes home.

I remember that plan worked out just as I had envisaged. As he had done for the past four days, as soon as my Mom's car had driven out, the door was opened by this man whose smell I did not like. I lunged at him as he entered. He got a very big fright, screamed, and backed away from the front door, far enough for me to run past him into the garden by the water.

I could sense the thunderstorm was brewing and it was going to be a nasty one. Miles was in a blind panic because he knew he had to get me back inside my cottage or his secret would be discovered and all hell would break loose. He tried everything to get me back into the cottage. Every time he came near me, I would bolt. In the end, to make sure he couldn't catch me, I ran into the water at the bottom of the garden and swam to the next door neighbour's yard.

There I stayed unseen, until Miles gave up, got the man out our cottage, locked up and went to his own cottage to escape the horrible storm. I remember that experience very clearly.

Never in my life, other than being at Adam, had I been so scared. It was the biggest electric storm I had ever experienced.

Tree branches were falling down around me. Lightening was striking the ground, the trees, the houses, the noise was deafening. The lake became like the ocean with waves and was not the calm peaceful lake Mom and I used to sit and watch the sun set on every night. It was being pounded by this storm. The wind was howling. The sky was pitch black and it was raining these hard white balls which were pelting my coat. This was truly a horrible experience and I remember wishing I was safely in our cottage, but I had to do this or my Mom will never know what is going on.

The storm went on forever. I really don't remember how long it lasted but for me, it was hours. Once things had calmed down, I was tempted to make my way back home, but didn't want to be caught by Miles. So I stayed put. I heard my Moms car pulling into the garage, I waited a few minutes to allow her time to go through all the doors, and I swam back home.

As she was coming down the stairs, I rounded the corner soaked to the bone. She got such a fright 'Finley! What the hell? Why are you outside? How? What on earth is going on? Are you OK? You soaked' she was rambling. It would take a little while for the penny to drop.

The rain water had made its way under our front door and into the cottage. Mom had a big job ahead of her and was in a state of shock not only about our flooded cottage, but the fact I was outside and not in the house where she had left me.

She kept mumbling to herself while she mopped up the water in the house. Once that was all done and I was dried off, she made a cup of tea and sat down. 'Finley, what the hell is going on? I left you inside for your own safety. I come home and you outside, soaked to the bone with leaves and sticks in your coat. So you have obviously been in the lake. I am so confused.

Finley did someone open this front door and let you out?' she asked me. I had one way of answering and that was by barking.

'OK! So someone opened the door?' she asked. 'Yes' I barked. 'Was it Jason?' she asked. I just kept quiet. 'OK, so it wasn't Jason. Was it Miles?' She continued knowing it was either Jason or Miles because she had Harpers key 'Yes' I barked. 'Finley are you sure it was Miles? Be very sure Finley before I make a scene for nothing' she insisted. 'Yes, yes, yes' I barked over and over. 'You such a clever boy. Thank you Foo. We have a problem. How the hell do I sort this out?' She was talking to herself.

She pulled her phone out and called Harper. 'Harper, I am sorry to be a pain, but I believe Miles is coming into my cottage when I am at work. Today I left Finley in the cottage because I knew the storm was on its way. I didn't want him outside. I came home to find him soaked in leaves, brambles and twigs. Someone has been into my cottage and as I have your key, that leaves Jason and Miles. I don't actually care which one of them it is, I am not happy about this'

Harper was shocked and said that Jason and Miles would never do something like that. Neither of them would ever go into our cottage. She said to Mom 'You must be mistaken. You must have left Finley outside when you left for work and you just not remembering. No one would go into your cottage girl. Definitely not Jason, and Miles has worked for us for fifteen years and has never put a foot out of place. I just can't see it girl.' She went on to tell Mom 'I will phone Jason now and check to see if he had to go into the cottage for any reason and then I will phone Miles and get back to you.'

Mom was not happy. She was not losing her mind, she knew and I knew, she had left me inside. She believed me when I told her it was Miles. Well, it wasn't Miles exactly, he was opening the door for his friend but I had no way of explaining that. So for me, the buck stopped at Miles.

A while later Harper called back 'Chick I have spoken to both Jason and Miles and both are adamant they have never gone into your cottage. Jason said he would never do something like that because he is terrified of Finley and you paying rent for that cottage. He would call you beforehand. Miles says, he didn't do it either. So chick, I am really thinking that you have made a mistake. You left Fin outside or he slipped out without you seeing him.'

My Mom was not impressed. So she devised a plan which she shared with Harper on the phone later that evening. She was going to set some low-tech traps over the next three days. She needed to leave things as they were and didn't want to raise suspicion with Miles. He knew that I stayed out all day with him until Mom came home. So following day, the sun was out, and I had gardening to do with Miles to clean up the mess from the storm. Mom secured slips of paper in the door frame so that when the door was opened after she had locked it, the paper would fall to the floor. There was no other way for the paper to fall. She checked it over and over and it was a good trap.

That following morning she set her trap, after looking around to see no one was watching. She felt with her fingers at the top of the door to see if she could still feel the edges of the paper and the paper was securely trapped by the door. When she returned from work she felt nothing when checking from the outside. So she gently opened the door, watching for the pieces of paper to fall, and nothing. When she opened the door completely, they were lying up the passage way.

Next day, she used my tennis ball. As she was closing the door she lay the ball against the door on the inside. This took some ingenuity because she was dressed for work in a pencil skirt and lying on the floor outside the front door so she could get the ball as close to the closed door as possible.

When she came home that afternoon the tennis ball was in the lounge. She also put a shoe in her bedroom against the closed door. So when you opened the bedroom door, the shoe would be pushed away from the door and she would know. Gosh she had so many things set up in the house to check every room. Little things that unless you had seen her do it, you would never know and without thinking, just step on it, or move it. She had taken photos of every little trick so she could be 100% that it had moved or was not in the exact place.

All this time, I knew Miles's friend was going in and I knew when Mom got home he was failing all her Ninja tests but I stayed out the way and just let this friend make all the mistakes because they would soon be caught.

After three days of this, she phoned Harper and forwarded the photos she had taken. Harper was in shock and very apologetic. She said she would take the key off Miles which she should have done in the beginning. My Mom told her not to bother because we were leaving for Durban in a few days' time. Besides, Miles now knew, that she knew, he was opening up and she didn't want trouble with Miles or his friends.

Instead she confided in her boss and he allowed her to take unpaid leave so she could pack up and not have the worry of people going into our cottage during the day. Knowing now that strangers had access to our little home, she bought a pepper spray gun and that, along with me, was our security. At least she had a little something for self-defense.

Those last few days we tried to enjoy as much as possible. It would be the last time we ever saw that house. Harper came over to visit that last evening and her, and Mom were sitting having a whisky in our usual spot and watching the sun set on the water when Harper said 'Danny, you and Finley have changed the energy of this property. It has been standing empty since we finished building it which is over two years ago. Since you and Finley moved in, everyone that comes to view it during the day, is in love with it. The whole energy of this property has changed and thank you so much Chick. You both turned all this brick and mortar into a home. I am so very sorry you had to go through what you did with Miles.'

Mom and I were only too grateful, we had somewhere to move to when it all went so wrong with Adam. Her, and Harper hugged and Mom said 'Thank you for everything. Forget about Miles. What he did was wrong, but aside from the last two weeks of a little drama, it has been amazing living here. It allowed both Fin and I to heal and I have learnt so much about myself.'

With that all said and done, our goodbyes were made the following day to Miles and Harper. The car was packed, only this time, everything mom had bought to make our cottage more 'homely' she gave to Miles to furnish his cottage out along with an envelope of money as a small thank you for taking care of me.

I could sense he was feeling very guilty for doing what he had done. He would never confess to mom, but his whole energy was saying, 'I am so sorry Miss Danny.' She thanked Miles very much for looking after me and wished him the best for his future. Miles shook her hand and thanked her very much for everything she had given him.

With the car a lot less full I had ample space to lie down and enjoy the next six hours on the road back to Durban. Only this time we were moving to Lala, my Gramps Mother who lived in Hillcrest. Mom tooted her horn and waved goodbye. I barked from the boot, and we were off.

Chapter 6

The drive to Natal was long. There was a throbbing heat, and even with the back windows open, and my ears blowing in the wind, it was damn hot and very sweaty. But it was a beautiful trip all the same. The first half of the drive was very flat with not that much to look at. Once you reach the half way mark and begin to enter Kwa Zulu Natal that is when things begin to change.

As you approach Harrismith which is considered half way, if you look on your right, you see the towering crags of the Drakensberg Mountains. That is truly impressive. Mom was telling me while driving 'Finley those mountains are probably 200 million years old if not more. Gosh, imagine how many stories they could tell us. Do you know Fin they stretch for more than 600 miles? I won't bore you with the history, but just look at how majestic they are. One day I will take you there and together we can climb one' that sounded like a great idea to me. I had never climbed a mountain before.

At the service station nestled in the foothills of the Drakensberg, we stopped and Mom opened the boot and let me out to stretch my legs. She also went into the local shop and bought us both loads of Biltong which is a dried meat similar to Jerky for the next leg of our journey. I did my business, drank some water from my travel bowl and back in the boot I hopped.

Not long after you drive through Harrismith you reach Van Reenens Pass. This was a very tricky part of the journey Mom was explaining. 'So many people don't realise how steep, narrow and bendy the road is. They come speeding down here fly off the edge, falling 1690m to their death. This is a pass through the Drakensberg Mountains. This road you must be driven with respect. Also Fin, in a few minutes you will see the weather changes. It's incredible, but from us driving all this time in the midday sun, it suddenly becomes chilly and so misty that you struggle to see the car in front of you. So people will drive with their hazard lights on.'

She wasn't kidding. The view of the Mountain range was lost within minutes after her last sentence. We slowed right down, Mom put her fog lights on, switched the music off, hazard lights went on, and all her concentration lay on the road ahead. We drove like this for a good half an hour before the mist began to clear and the drive returned to normal. I had seen enough and decided I was going to have a nap and leave Mom to it.

I remember we did one other stop for me to stretch my legs and when I jumped back in the boot she said 'Next stop is Lala Fin, not too long to go now' Boy was I happy to hear that. Although I was comfortable, I was tired of the car and just wanted to get out and not have to climb back in.

Finally we arrived at Lala. I was about to meet my Gramps Mother. The electric gate opened and we drove down this long driveway and stopped outside a double story house, hidden among all the tall trees. Out the front door came Lala smiling. I instantly liked her. Wow! She had a great smell.

After all the greetings had taken place and I had gushed over Lala making her laugh, we unpacked the car, and began to make ourselves at home for the third time in as many months! Lala had a simple, yet beautiful home which my Gramps, Dad had built with his own hands, many years ago. It wasn't the biggest house I had seen, but it was lovely. It had this huge porch off the lounge that stretched the length of the house and upstairs off both the bedrooms was a veranda the same length as the porch.

The house was filled with lots of good smells. I remember thinking 'Now this is what a home should smell like!'

We had what was left of the weekend with Lala and then it was business as usual. Only this time, I had Lala to spend my days with. Lala used to tell me stories and sometimes read to me from Thomas Merton's books. I don't remember most of it to be fair, but I do remember he was a Trappist Monk who mostly wrote on spirituality, social justice and Lala loved his writing. She used to tell me that my Mom had 'soul'

Those first few weeks flew by. Mom would go to work, I would wonder around our five acre ground, lie out on the porch, or rest on the carpet in the lounge while Lala read her book to me. They were easy days. I did notice and so did Mom that Lala was struggling with the stairs. She was already in her mid-80's and although still a very fit woman, her hip joints used to give her quite a bit of pain and she would hold onto the bannister going up the stairs and inevitably had to stop a couple of times before reaching the top.

The family were a little concerned and wanted her to move to single story bungalow that was closer to where other family members lived. That way, they could keep a closer eye on her.

Lala didn't want to move though. She was happy in her home and always said it was wonderful having Mom and I. Lala and Mom would spend hours at night talking about life, those that were suffering, relationships, theological speculations, non-sentient beings like plants, Karma, life and death, reincarnation and so much more. Mom adored Lala and found her to be a wealth of spiritual knowledge.

For the first few weeks, everything in Moms life was work, work, and more work. The minute she got home, she would put her handbag down, change shoes, and off we would go on our walks while Lala finished heating dinner up. I found the dogs in this area a lot friendlier. Strangely, all the dogs in this area were much loved and a part of their family. Very different to Witbank.

Where we lived was a big farming community and there were loads of monkeys. I had never seen a monkey before and boy are they cheeky. They would constantly scream, shout and grunt at me. I started out chasing them, but they were quick! They would wait until I was almost on top of them and then effortlessly just jump into the nearest tree and shout 'Come doggie. What? You can't climb a simple tree? Ahhh the doggie can't climb a tree!' They would all laugh their heads off at my feeble attempt at tree climbing. Other days, they would tease me by picking mangos and throwing them at me. I vowed to get even with those monkeys, but I never did. They were far too quick and far too smart. They out foxed me every time.

Instead, I made friends with a horse called Sunny Banana. She lived a few houses away from Lala and I liked her immediately. She also got teased by the Monkeys but they had grown bored of her now. Mom used to take carrots and apples for Sunny Banana and we used to have long conversations while she munched on her treats.

She used to be a work horse on a farm close to those mountains we passed on our way to Durban. Sunny Banana had been rescued. She was old now and allowed to live her days out chewing on fruit, veg and other delicious treats.

She told me the people who owned her now were very kind to her and took great care of her. No one was allowed to ride her anymore, and she was free. Once she had finished her treats, we would chase each other up and down the length of the property. That first day she started out with a clippity-clop but Sunny Banana soon realized if she wanted to compete with me, she had to put some horse into that! The old girl was fast, but not as quick as me.

Mom would stand there laughing and watching us running up and down the wire. Eventually we had to leave and finish our walk around the big cul-de-sac of farm houses because Lala would be waiting with dinner. The walk usually took us 30 minutes. I would say goodbye to Sunny Banana and tease her 'See you tomorrow slow coach' and she would neigh loudly and stand so tall on her back legs.

I really liked that horse so much and the feeling was mutual. Of all the friends to make, it had to be a horse. So that became our nightly ritual. Always a walk after work, and always challenging and competing against Sunny Banana.

A few times Mom would leave me with Lala while she visited her two dearest friends, Austin and Cooper. They owned an antique shop in Hillcrest which had been going for thirty years now. Actually almost the same length of time, they had been a couple. Mom often spoke about them, and she loved those blokes very much.

Mom was telling Lala that she had known 'the boys' her words not mine, for 25 years. My Nan and my Gramps, used to own a little art and craft shop next door to them for a few years. It was visiting my Nan at the shop one day when my Mom was in her twenties that she met the boys and it was love at first sight for the three of them. They were soul mates, mom would say.

Our life was going really well. Yes we had some scary nights but they were not as frequent or intense as the ones we had experienced with Adam in Witbank or at Harper's cottage on the lake.

Mom often said to Lala 'Gosh Lala, I cannot believe you have lived on this big property all by yourself and you not scared' Lala would reply with 'Well, once your Grandad died, it became very lonely. I have been very happy here Danny but I am finding the stairs a bit of a challenge now.

I don't really want to leave here because of all my happy memories. There have been many times over the years that I have felt unsafe, but God has looked after me. To be honest the thing I miss is my car and not being able to drive myself to the shops. Before you arrived, I had to rely on your Aunty Ivy to take me shopping. I gave my car up and cancelled my license because let's face it, I am getting a bit old to be on the roads and if I caused an accident, I would never forgive myself. So I removed all temptation. To be fair, aside from the grocery side of things and being able to wonder around the shopping center at my leisure, I am quite content '

We were very happy at Lala. Mom and I had a lovely big double bedroom with a bathroom en suit and the balcony which I loved to sleep on at night. I felt safe because it was so high and I could see across the valley, right down to the Kloof Gorge which was a nature reserve.

Urgh as it always does, things just all seemed to happen again at once. Mom got a phone call from Adam, who apologized and asked Mom to forgive him. She told him in time she would forgave him but she would never forget what he did. He for the first time didn't argue back and went on to explain he had to postpone his wedding because of some drama in his life, but it was all back on track and he wanted to know if Mom would fly up for the big day. He also said that he would transfer Ann's car which we were still driving, into Moms name and she was responsible for the payments, tax and insurance, which she was very grateful for.

Mom apologized, but declined flying up for the wedding saying 'Dad, I am sorry, but I am so busy at work, and I cannot leave Lala alone with Finley. It's just not fair on her. I will be with you in spirit and I really do hope you have a wonderful day.' He was very disappointed but seemed to understand. He never said his usual 'that bloody dog rules your life' so maybe he had learnt some humility in our absence as Mom said.

Next the phone beeped and it was a message from Ryan the narcissist. Now that message, I was not happy to see come through. I thought we had got rid of him, but he was telling Mom how much he missed her, and that if she had just done this, and that, or not said this, or that, everything would be fine. From over 9000 miles, he was still blaming and manipulating her. Unfortunately for him though, Mom had toughened up and his messages had no effect on her at all.

Then the next day the phone rang and it was Steve. He was very sick and needed a quadruple bi-pass. He would have to get through the next two months until June when he would be admitted. His surgeon was going on leave, and Steve was asked to hold out using a spray called Glyceryl Trinitrate until he returned. This spray he was told, was to be used when he felt an episode coming on. It was to be sprayed under his tongue to widen the blood vessels in the heart. The spray would make him feel very woozy and so ideally he needed to be sitting when using it. The Surgeon felt confident that it would buy the needed time until he returned. If however, Steve's condition worsened during that time, he was to admit himself immediately.

We were all very concerned about Steve. Mom begged him to keep in touch and to please put her name down as a next of kin or a second contact, so she could phone and check up on his progress once he went into hospital. He said he would.

Then the biggest blow for us that week was Lala saying 'Danny, after numerous conversations with Aunty Ivy, and giving it much thought, I have decided it is time for me to move to a bungalow. Aunty Ivy has found me a lovely bungalow just down the road from here, you could walk there if you wanted. It's a lovely two bedroom unit with a garden, and no stairs. I really am beginning to take strain. The toilets are upstairs and I am up and down several times a day and its killing me. I am so sorry my girl, but don't worry, you and Finley can stay here for as long as you like. There is no time restraint on you at all. This house is yours for as long as you both need it'

Oh shucks! Things were changing again and I was very sad to hear Lala was moving out even if it was just down the road. Not only would I miss her reading to me every day, but I was now going to be all alone while Mom was at work. Next month being May, Lala would move. So our days were now spent packing boxes until Mom returned home from work and it was time to race against Sunny Banana and snub those annoying monkeys.

Chapter 7

The day came for Lala to move out. She had told Mom she would leave some furniture for us so we didn't have to start from scratch. The main things, she would take but she would leave our bed, a spare sofa, bits in the kitchen and other odds and ends. Mom said she would take half a day's leave to help out and get me out the way, but Lala said it was no problem because she had furniture removals and there really wasn't anything Mom could do to help.

So that day, to get me out the way and preserve the mover's bums from my nipping, she took me to the office with her. That was fun. I got to see who she worked with and everyone liked me very much. They had all heard so much about me and now they were finally meeting me. I got very spoilt with sandwiches, chunks of biltong and a few sugary sweets. After wondering around the office and greeting everyone, I lay in her office under her desk and made sure no one came in!

Mom did leave early that day because she was uncomfortable not being at the house to help Lala. So just after lunch, she packed up in the office, we said our goodbyes and headed on the forty minute journey back home. We arrived there pretty much at the same time the truck was pulling out the driveway.

I stayed in the car so Mom could make sure the coast was clear of anyone I didn't know and who I could give a hard time to. Only Aunty Ivy was at the house and she was about to lock up and allow the man in the truck to follow her to Lala's new address.

A few brief words were exchanged, goodbyes made at the front door, and the whole place fell empty and silent. Mom opened the back car door and I jumped out. When she opened the front door, she couldn't believe her eyes. The house was completely empty and very dirty from where furniture had been standing for years which is to be expected.

The removers had taken everything. Either Lala, Aunty Ivy, or both had forgotten to remind the removers to leave the pieces of furniture promised. So what we had left was an old steel table outside on the porch with two falling apart wicker chairs. An old wooden table in the kitchen with a blue checked table cloth, a few old bits and pieces in the kitchen cupboards, and an old thread bare, tatty wicker sofa on the upstairs balcony. All the curtains had been taken. We were back to being like goldfish in a bowl mom muttered to herself. She didn't want to phone Lala or Aunty Ivy and moan, she was only too grateful that we still had a roof over our head. So she just got on with it.

A couple of weeks back, the boxes that Mom and Steve had packed in England were delivered. Her company had kept the boxes in storage until she had a place to deliver them. All 27 boxes Mom had piled in Lala's unused garage. I had my bed on the floor but Mom didn't even have a blanket to sleep on. That's when she said, 'it's time to open a few of those boxes Fin'

On the way to the garage, she spotted an old discarded outdoor broom with a broken shaft. She was so happy to have found that. Back inside we went where she swept up many years of dust and dirt. The whole cottage was given a once over and using her hands, she scooped up all the dirt onto newspaper, rolled it up and threw it away.

Fortunately she had labelled all the boxes so she knew which ones to open and which ones to leave shut. One of the boxes she opened had my old brass toy box in. She had bought that in a charity store back in England. I was so happy to have my toy box back. In there were all my fluffy toys, my tennis balls, old bones I had kept, an old slipper of moms I had chewed when I was a puppy, a pigs ear and some squeaky plastic toys. It was fantastic for me.

Next up was 'bedroom' stuff. Mom pulled out her old duvet, pillows, and other little bits and pieces. She also opened the box labelled clothing because winter was setting in and it was becoming really very cold at night. It often went down to zero and Mom had been threatening to open the clothing box with jerseys in, but hadn't gotten around to it. South Africa doesn't have central heating. Most people will use little gas heaters and those Lala had taken.

She was going to need all the clothes she could get her hands on because we were now both sleeping in an empty house on natural stone flooring which was great for the summer months because it was lovely and cool, but for the winter nights we were now experiencing, it was like sleeping in a fridge.

After first laying down a few jerseys on the cold floor, she took her king size duvet, folded it in half and put a pillow up at the top. Her bed was made. My bed she placed on top of my old sheep skin which had been found in one of the boxes. It was too small for Mom to sleep on, but my Snoozzee duvet fit perfectly on there and I was warm and comfortable.

That night, I remember Mom went to the service station and bought some junk food for our dinner. She had to wait for the shops to open in the morning to buy some proper food along with kitchen cleaning stuff and towels. Thank goodness she had kept the cooler box from Benoni because that was to become her fridge again.

It was a very cold and to be honest, an unpleasant night. There is something really quite unsettling about sleeping in a house that is empty and has no curtains. You hear every twig that falls to the ground. So I was on red alert all night. Following morning we were both up before the birds and Mom found that old camping kettle she had taken from Adam, and made herself a cup of tea before getting ready for work.

'Fin, I have to go to work today. I am going to try and leave early so I can buy us some groceries. You will have to stay here please. I need you to keep our house safe. I am going to leave the lounge door open to the garden so you can lie inside or outside, which ever you feel safer doing. I will be back as soon as my meetings are over and I have done some shopping. See you in 5 minutes Foo. Love you' and off she drove down the long driveway.

It was unheard of in Hillcrest that you leave your house open and go to work, but Mom really didn't want me outside all day on my own. So she locked the gate on the staircase leading to the bedrooms, set the alarm for the upstairs part of the house and decided to take a chance on the rest of it. Besides, I would guard that.

The day wasn't too bad to be fair. I lay outside on the porch, chatted through the hedges to the neighbour's dogs and generally got the low down on the area from them. Having the company of three huge German Shepherds through the thick hedge, made the world of difference. They told me that I need to be alert at all times because their house had been broken into many times and although they had tried very hard to protect their property, there were a couple of occasions that even they, had failed.

Their stories did not sit easy with me. It was scary listening to what they had lived through. I really wanted to just go back to England. Go visit my Nan and Gordie, walk through the woodlands, chase squirrels again and sleep well at night. How I prayed that would happen. Gee I even missed Gordies history lectures and that is saying something! You know you desperate when you miss Gordies long stories on Picts, Druids, Gaels, and Romans! I was definitely losing my mind. Most definitely.

Mom came home later that day with all her goodies and although we were in an empty house, we made the best of what we had. The following night, Austin and Cooper decided to give Mom a surprise visit and came over with two bottles of wine and a bunch of flowers. It was the first time I had met them, and they became my heroes. I liked them from the time they climbed out their 4x4.

They smelt of dog and had a great scent. I would learn they had six German Shepherds on their farm. They were mortified on entering the house and seeing how Mom and I were living. Mom told them 'Calm down. It's not important. We have a roof over our head, and I will at some point, get around to furnishing the house. It's only been a few days like this and when I am not so busy and can take a bit of time off work, I will shop for furniture. Now sit down and open that bottle of wine will you!'

With that, the four of us sat on the stone floor, I lay listening to the conversation while they laughed and shared the two bottles of wine. They were very loath to leave Mom and begged her to please go with them to the farm and sleep in a bed. She said no because she had to be at the office by eight and we were just fine. They had to stop their fretting.

Following night, Austin and Cooper were back at the gate ringing the bell, only this time with a double bed mattress, linen, pillows, a lampshade, some bedroom curtains, a thick blanket, a TV that had a built in DVD player, a brand new in the box 12 piece dinner service, and a whole load of movies.

'Bless your hearts. Thank you so much guys. You really didn't need to do this, we honestly are fine, but thank you. Wow Fin! We have curtains! And we can watch movies in bed tonight on our double bed mattress with our new cushy linen, fluffy blanket, and a side lamp too boot. What a treat!' she said while laughing with the boys.

More wine was drunk, more laughing and sharing life experiences exchanged, and it was off to our bedroom with curtains, and a comfy bed that Mom and I would share. We didn't watch movies that night, we were too tired.

Over the next couple of weeks, more calls came in from Steve who was not well at all and beginning to doubt he would make it for another month. Ryan also sent a few more messages to Mom testing the water and asking her if he could come over on a holiday and spend some time with her.

She told him 'No Ryan, it's going on three years that I have been alone and to be honest, I am happy with my own company.' It slowed the messages down, but it never stopped them completely. During one of those messages he told mom that the one cat had died. As horrible as it sounds, the death of the black cat called Star really didn't affect me. I had bad memories of those two fur balls.

Mom and I also went to many Flea Markets and she bought some lovely old persian carpets for the house. She also bought a beautiful antique four poster bed, side tables and other pieces of furniture from the boy's antique shop. Our little home was coming together nicely.

She bought two great sofas from a pawn shop. Instead of traditional curtains, she decided to go Moroccan with her furnishing and had beautiful Indian silk Saree's which she draped and pinned up in the windows. Steve had sent her from England some stunning Moroccan lamp shades and a fake chandelier for the entrance hall. When all the lamps were switched on at night, the house looked magical.

Austin and Cooper came over a couple of times during our refurbishment and were amazed at what Mom had done with the house. It really did look beautiful and the colours they said were 'breathtaking'. Our kitchen now had a super duper fridge and all the mod cons to make life easy. We had gone from the floor, to a fully furnished home that even I have to say, was really comfortable.

Even the garden Mom sorted out. She got garden services in to mow the lawn and tend to the garden and she planted beautiful ever greens and loads of colourful winter flowers. Lala and Aunty Ivy were amazed at what she had done to the property. Suddenly over a period of two months, the house had become a home and it had charm. The house was smiling again and so was I because I had a new friend Gracie.

Mom could see that I was lonely and taking a bit of strain during the day without any company. So she got hold of the Border Collie Rescue and that is how Gracie came into our lives. I loved Gracie at first sight. She had lived such an interesting life.

She told me she was originally from Scotland and had been brought over to South Africa for breeding purposes. Not long after arriving here, she had been stolen. Gracie ran away from her thieving new family the first chance she got and became a street dog. She did try for over a year to sniff her way back to the farm but it was impossible. In the end she gave up and lived with many people, but no one family in particular. She became everyone's part time dog until the rescue people found her wondering the streets and picked her up.

Gracie was smart, gifted and skilled. She knew how to survive and she had many stories to share with me. I was so happy for her company and my life changed so much after that. I was no longer on guard alone and Gracie loved my Mom very much. She would do anything for Mom and was incredibly obedient and loyal. She put to me to shame truth be told.

I introduced Gracie to Sunny Banana and she too began to race against her. Boy did we have fun. I hate to admit it, but Gracie was even faster than me. She could run like the wind and never seemed to tire. I on the other hand had to slow down because my leg began to play up and my heart felt like it was going to burst in my chest. Every now and then, my leg really aches and all that running trying to beat Gracie and Sunny Banana, was not doing me any favours. I did however lose 6 kg's from chasing Gracie and Sunny Banana. I became super fit and my heart gave up trying to burst on me!

Mom also felt safer at night with the two of us. Gracie could hear a pin drop a mile down the road. Together we would walk the perimeter of the garden in the evenings several times to make sure all was safe. I introduced her to the three German Shepherds through the hedge and the five of us would be on guard and exchanging details of the latest word on the street. So we were all kept informed. Bad news travelled fast through the dog network in that neighbourhood which was a good thing.

The time had come for Steve to go into Hospital. He had made it to early June and now it was all in the surgeons hands. I remember my Mom was worried sick about the operation. He was going into surgery early morning, and they had estimated the op would take around six hours. Well I remember Mom phoning every hour after the initial five hours and he was always in theatre.

I think he ended up being in theatre for something silly like eleven hours because they had complications. Along with the quadruple bi-pass they also ended up changing a valve while they had him open. I can't remember the exact details, but it was very serious.

The Hospital was not happy to give Mom any information, and so she said she was his wife. Which of course didn't match the details he had given prior to the op so I think they just humoured Mom after that. Meanwhile back in England my Moms sister Layla was phoning too and they wouldn't give her any information either, so she became his sister. When Steve was finally able to take a call on his mobile, he was laughing and saying he went into theatre a single man with a brother and came out with a wife and sister.

I heard Mom telling Nan that nine out of ten times, you are discharged within a few days and you go home to heal. Sadly, Steve was not one of those cases. Although an incredibly fit man in his fifties, it had gone a bit wrong for poor Steve. He had picked up a hospital bug and his one lung collapsed. So from that initial call where he laughed about his new wife and sister, he ended up fighting for his life.

Just short of three months later, he was finally discharged. He couldn't thank the St Thomas Hospital staff enough. They had fought hard, worked around the clock, they had saved his life and he was awfully grateful to each and every one of them.

He told Mom he was not allowed to fly for at least two months, but once he was given the all clear, he would be heading back to South Africa to get some sun on his skin and to relax. He asked if he could stay with us and Mom very quickly answered 'Yes of course!'

It was one of the evenings in June when Mom was talking to Gracie and I when she said 'I am missing the UK. I have such a lovely home now and it's ours for as long as we want it, but my heart for some strange reason is not here. I miss our walks in the woodlands, I miss Nana, and I miss our safe life. I took so much for granted. I complained daily. Always thinking the grass was greener on the other side. Gosh I wish I could wriggle my nose and get us out of here.'

I had been missing our home so much. Gracie, strangely enough understood how we felt. She had been very young when she left Scotland, but she still had very fond memories of being born there and would tell me the most amazing stories of the Highlands and what it was like in the winter which was when she was born. She used to tell me it was a truly magical place. The glistening ice and the wintry landscapes. The fluffy snow and the warmth of the log fire in the lounge where she and her siblings would sleep with her Mom and Dad. It all sounded wonderful to me. It was a world away from my experience with my Mother and siblings in a stinky wet and dark cage. But I too had fond memories myself of Mom throwing snow balls at me during our winters. Yes, I also wanted to go home. So I gave Mom a big barking session and she just smiled. She knew, I was agreeing with her.

However, our life was here now and for the foreseeable future at least. Mom had a good job, was earning a lot of money and had spent a fortune furnishing our home. I remember we went a few weekends to Austin and Cooper's Farm in the Drakensberg. That was incredible. Their house sat right at the top of the mountain and the view of the landscape was spectacular. They had built this house brick by brick over many years and it was stunning. Of course with them being antique dealers, their home inside was jaw dropping.

Their six German Shepherds scared the hell out of me initially. Gracie they accepted no problem, but me, they were a little more cautious of and it made me very nervous. Look they were nice dogs, but they did make a few threats that made me more than a little uncomfortable. I kept telling them, 'Guys, I am only here for the weekend and then I am going home. Relax! I am not here to stay.' I think my accent confused them too.

Grace and I had loads of fun. The cottage we all stayed in was called Beckett. When you entered Beckett, off the lounge was a porch where you had a view of the rambling Drakensberg mountain range. I remember Mom gasping at its beauty and telling us 'Look at all those wildflowers! Oh Fin and Gracie, look at the grasslands, the white berg lilies, the orchids, the butterflies. I used to think God came from North Wales, but maybe he comes from here. This is breathtakingly beautiful.'

Yes, it was stunning and I can't take that away from it, but the most important thing she had overlooked was a huge pond that Austin and Cooper had built many years ago. It was surrounded by greenery, had a water flowing feature, lilies floating in it and fish called Koi that swam peacefully all day long. That was about to end.

When Mom saw me eyeing out the pond she shouted 'Finley! No! No swimming in there. Those are expensive……' I was in the water before she had finished her sentence. I was fishing my heart out on the boy's expensive Koi. I remember they were really slippery things and hard as I tried, I couldn't catch one. I was even snorkelling at one point. My whole head was submerged trying to catch these slippery things. I had mom, Cooper and Austin all chasing me which was huge fun. I'd jump out the pond, race around Beckett and jump back in through the side under the hedges.

Then they would all jump in to pull me out, and I'd slip past them, do my victory lap and jump back in barking. Wow! That was a fun day for me. All three of them couldn't catch me and were falling and slipping on the wet rocks and I was having the time of my life. I remember Gracie standing there just watching and saying 'You are in such trouble Finley. Stop this bad behaviour. You behaving like a puppy!' I remember saying something like 'Whatever Gracie. I am having fun. Mind your own business'

After ages, I was caught by Cooper and my wet disobedient body, dragged out. My Mom was coming up with swear words I hadn't heard before. She was really angry with me for upsetting the apple cart with these fancy fish of the boys. She was frustrated and towel dried me with a vengeance. After that I was locked up in Beckett which I was least pleased about. Gracie was standing outside the window of the lounge saying 'You can't say I didn't warn you! You have brought this on yourself Finley.' I wasn't the least bit interested in what Gracie's opinion was so instead I asked her 'Gracie, how good are you at opening windows? You couldn't help me with this lounge one could you? Please?'

'No I couldn't Finley. I don't fancy spending my afternoon locked in Beckett with you. I am going to play with the German Shepherds. I will see you later when Mom decides to forgive you' and off she trotted, leaving me barking abuse at her.

Looking back, I must have driven Mom and the boy's crazy with that pond. As soon as the door was opened, I was out, running at full speed, and jumping straight back into the forbidden pond.

In the end the boys decided they would remove the Koi and put them in their other large pond. Well, it wasn't a pond, they had converted their swimming pool into a koi haven. The swimming pool was off their lounge, secluded and fenced off with wooden panels. It had huge palms that cast shadows on the water and relief from the sun. I heard Cooper saying to Mom 'He is a little shit! But at least here, he won't be able to get to the fish.'

While I was locked up, I watched Cooper, catching one big fish at a time. Putting it in a bucket and walking to the pool which I had no access to. There he would tip the bucket and the fish would flop out into the pool water. Once the last of the expensive slipperies had been removed, the door was opened and within a flash, I was back in that pond. Gracie wanted nothing to do with me. I called her so many times and told her it's such fun, but she was a goodie two shoes and would never do anything to upset Mom.

The boys had left behind a few inexpensive fish for me to try and catch. That pond kept me busy for hours on end. I was now in disfavour with Gracie, so she played with the German Shepherds and I fished all day on my own.

That evening Gracie said to me 'Finley, I am being serious now. You causing a lot of trouble with that pond. You need to give it a break. Come and investigate the farm with us tomorrow. There has to be something else you can do other than causing chaos and stress for everyone. You not being fair on Mom.' She was right, I knew that, even though I remember never admitting to that.

With Gracies words still ringing in my ears while I was falling asleep on the bed next to Mom, I decided I was not going to risk being locked up again. I would take her advice and look for other things I could chase and play with and I would find them when the sun decided to wake up and pull the duvet from its face.

Finally it was morning and Mom, Gracie and I walked onto the porch to have our tea and toast. I left my last piece of toast for Gracie, I had a busy day ahead of me. As I walked off Gracie barked 'Finley, behave yourself! Stay out of trouble today'

'Gimme a break will you Gracie!' I barked back at her and with that, I wondered off to see what other treasures the boys had hidden on the top of this mountain. It didn't take me long and I found the perfect thing to chase and keep me entertained. A thing I later learned was a Rooster, whose name was Rooster. Man was that bird stupid and fun to chase. I thought all birds could fly but this Rooster had wings that clearly didn't work. I will say this, the Rooster was fast on his two legs.

All the birds I had chased in England could more or less fly. I could chase them so far, and they would just fly off into a tree and cling onto a branch. This Roosters wings were for show. I only found out listening to Mom and the boys through peals of laughter, saying 'Poor Rooster. Finley must wonder what type of bird this is that doesn't fly. He doesn't understand that chickens and roosters don't fly'

They don't? Cool! I would make a mental note to find more of these rooster birds to chase. I kept wondering why we had never come across these birds that don't fly in England. Oh well. Doesn't matter, I had a whole cage of these birds with wings for show, to chase around the garden.

That morning after chasing rooster around the garden for ages, Austin appeared out of nowhere and rooster threw himself into the safety of Austin's arms and it was game over. Then my Mom appeared and then Cooper and of course moaning Gracie. They had all witnessed the last leg of this rooster running for its life and jumping into Austin's arms. I remember them all trying to be very serious and reprimand me, but in the end they couldn't hold out and they were crying with laughter.

Rooster was safe and sound and had, had enough exercise to last him a life time. Austin carried the worn out fellow who was shouting obscenities at me and put him back in with his harem while my Mom pulled one of Roosters tail feathers from my mouth.

Another game over for me. So now I was not allowed to Koi fish and I was not allowed to chase Rooster or any of his harem chicks. I would have to find something else to do. That afternoon after we all went for a long walk over the Drakensberg mountains Cooper started a BBQ.

Out came Austin with two really big cages with these two huge birds inside. I was told they Parrots. One was an African Grey called Pebbles and the other was a white Cockatoo called Kipling. Austin laughingly told Mom, 'For their own safety I am going to leave them in their cage'

I walked slowly up to the cage with the African Grey called Pebbles. As I started sniffing around the cage Pebbles shouted loudly in Cooper's voice 'Fuck off!' Boy did I get a fright, I jumped back knocking Moms wine over and falling on top of Shadow the eldest German Shepherd and leader of the pack who was not impressed. 'Easy boy! I was resting. You don't want to upset those two birds. They are not to be messed with'

Once I had gathered myself together again, and the laughter from Mom and the boys had calmed down. I asked Shadow 'How come these birds talks human? Where I come from, the birds don't talk human' Shadow was old and a bit irritated because I had disturbed his afternoon nap but gave me an answer all the same.

'These birds talk human, they talk dog. In fact they talk many languages and are very clever. Sometimes, I think my Dad is calling me, I stop what I am doing, run all the way back home only to be laughed at and called an idiot by either Pebbles or Kipling. It's all a game for them. They actually a bloody pain, but my Dads love them. Problem is they sound exactly like my Dads. I can't ignore the call because I never know if it's them messing with me, or my actual Dad calling me' he went on to tell me they have even caused arguments in the house because they repeat things they have heard throughout the day.

This was incredible for me. Birds that talk so many languages. I decided it was best I stay well away from these two talking birds who tattletale. So I didn't sniff the cage again and I gave them both a wide berth.

I have such fond memories of our weekends at the boys. I was always sad to leave there. So many interesting things to see, do and chase.

I remember our weeks turned to months and then one evening out the blue, Mom made an announcement to Gracie and I.

Chapter 8

'We going home. I cannot live like this anymore. Driving home I narrowly escaped with my life. There was a shootout on Fields Hill and so many cars were hit by flying bullets. People shot dead, others injured. This was once a beautiful Country but I'm afraid for me, it's no longer a safe place to live. I think it's time to pack up and head back to England. How we are going to do this, I really don't know yet. I will take you and Gracie to the Vet so we can get that Rabies Serology done and get Gracie her passport, and I will make a plan for us to return.'

This was the best news ever. Gracie and I spoke about it all night. We were so happy and Gracie was so excited to be going back to England. We had one job as far as we were concerned, and that was to keep Mom and ourselves safe until we all flew out.

I shared all my stories of the flight over with Gracie and told her about that stinky stuff they spray in the box. She had vague memories of a similar experience when she left Scotland for South Africa as a young puppy. Nothing I said put her off. She just wanted to meet the squirrels, walk in the woodlands, go swimming in the lake, and meet Nan, Gramps and Gordie. That night, I don't think we slept much. Between guarding the house and exchanging stories, we were exhausted in the morning.

Sunny Banana didn't take the news very well. She was so sad that we were not going to be living down the road from her for much longer. Poor Sunny, would have no one to race against, and who was going to bring her apples and carrots when we left? Both Gracie and I tried really hard to cheer her up and Gracie even let her win a few races. Nothing seemed to cheer up Sunny Banana.

A few days after Moms decision, Steve now out of hospital and recovering well, phoned and said he would be arriving next month which was November. He would stay with us for a month and then head home. Mom told him 'Steve, we going back to the UK. My mind is made up. Every day I am living on my nerves edge. The crime here is out of control. It's no life living in fear day in and day out. When Finley and Gracie start barking early hours of the morning, my heart literally stops. I wonder every time it happens, is tonight my last night alive? The WhatsApp group that I am on for this area, just doesn't stop. Houses are being robbed, people held at gun point, dogs poisoned and electric gates jammed open, on an almost daily basis. This house in all honesty, must be the only one in the cul-de-sac that hasn't been targeted. Our luck is bound to run out at some point. I just can't do it anymore.'

Steve asked Mom when she planned on returning and what her plans were and she told him 'Well, It's mid-October now. You coming for the month of November. It takes three months for the dogs Serology tests to return. So, if I get those bloody test done this week, we looking at November, December and January. I will hand my notice in at the beginning of January. Take the month of February to pack and sort all of us out, and I plan to be back in England for Fin and my birthday in March'

I remember Gracie and I were in shock. Wow! It wouldn't be long and we would be flying back home. We were surprised at how much strain Mom had been taking. I remember us looking at each other and feeling awful. We didn't enjoy scaring her with our barking, but we had to do it. As I said, the German Shepherds next door, kept us in the dog loop and we were always told when trouble was near and the only way to warn Mom was to bark and let her know it's time to lock the house up.

Most evenings after our walk and race against Sunny Banana, she would sit outside on the porch with music playing and have a drink. On the odd night the Shepherds would warn us to get inside there were threats further up the road and heading our way. So we would then have to warn Mom. No more sitting on the veranda. Hurry up! Get inside and lock all the security gates.

We would put on a good display of barking in unison, and she knew immediately, that we were trying to warn her. She would say 'Thanks guys, lets wrap it up and get inside. Be on alert you two' with that she would grab her smokes, her wine, switch the music off, lock the sliding doors to the porch and then pull shut and lock the heavy security trelli door.

After that, we would all just stay quiet, and wait for the danger to pass. The Shepherds would let Grace and I know when the coast was clear and to show Mom it was over, we would start a game of tug of war and play fight. Danger had decided to pass our home thanks to God and Anubis.

Next up was our trip to the Vet. That was a horrible day and one I still remember today very vividly. It was to be the day we would find out that Gracie, simply couldn't return to England with us.

My visit with the Vet was all straight forward. My Mom has a folder labelled 'Finley Doc's' and in there is my passport, my Veterinary Card from England and all other documents relating to my travel into South Africa. Everything was in order. It all matched. Every vaccination I had was reported in my card. Details of my operation on my leg, X-rays, the lot. There were no gaps in my history at all.

So for me, it was a simple case of in and out. All the Vets always remarked on how well behaved I was. When asked to sit, I sat. I would give my paw for them to draw blood, and would stand still for my injections. I always earned my sweet at the end of my appointment and Mom was always very proud. All the Vets without exception would say 'What an incredible boy he is. I have never in all my career, had a dog lift his paw, allow me to shave a spot on his leg, and draw his blood without any fuss whatsoever. Incredible!'

Once I was done, it was now Gracie's turn. Mom said to the Vet 'Doc, I only got Gracie two months ago. I was given this sheet of paper with her details on. I want to take her back with us to the UK, and I need Gracie brought up to speed as quickly as you can. I believe all her information should be on her chip.'

It wasn't long and the man said 'Sorry Danny, but the papers don't match the dog. I can only think these papers belong to another dog. All the information you have supplied me does not match. I know the kennels you got Gracie from very well. We do all their work for them and they are a reputable organisation. If I hadn't checked myself, I would say this dog was stolen by you.'

'What? Are you crazy? I got her from Diane, along with this thoroughbred certificate. Phone Diane and speak to her yourself.' Mom said

'As I said to you Danny, had I not checked myself, I would think you have stolen this dog. I have already spoken to Diane and she has confirmed everything you told me. She is also mistaken thinking these papers belong to this dog. There is no history on this dog. The details on her chip are outdated and no one has ever changed them. So basically we have no idea if she has ever even been dewormed. Has she had all her vaccinations? We don't know. You call her Gracie, but that is not the name on her chip. To get this dog flight ready, will take at least a year. England are very strict and everything needs to match, and all the dots need to join. This is going to be a long process Danny.'

'I don't understand. What do you mean the details on the chip don't match and what name do you have for this poor girl?' asked Mom

'Sorry Danny, I cannot disclose that information because you are not the legal owner according to her chip. Having said that and while we have been talking I asked reception to try and trace the person on her chip and it's a dead end. Now we can sort this all out for you. There are ways to sort this out. All I am saying, is with Gracie now having no history at all, we have to start from the beginning. So from her very first puppy injection, and work our way through to a serology test and her being able to fly. You say you leaving in three or four months, and I am saying, she will not be going with you. After her first injection she has to wait for 6 months before we give her the next injection. Does this all make sense now?' He asked Mom

'No it doesn't! There must be something you can do to make sure I can fly out with Gracie in a few months' time. Surely to God you can make it happen. Please, I am begging you.' Mom cried out.

Turned out, according to the Vet, there was nothing he could do. Rules were rules and he was not about the break them for one dog. We were all devastated. Mom, Gracie and myself, pretty much cried the whole way home. What now?

That evening Mom was sobbing on the phone to the boys and telling them the story. Cooper said 'Sweetie, listen to me. My niece has a crocodile farm in the Drakensberg. She had two Collies but one recently died of old age. She has one young girl and has been wanting to get a friend for Holly for ages now. Gracie will love Shelly and to be honest, she would be going to a home that would adore her. She will have the same life as she does with you. Holly sleeps inside, on the sofa, on the beds, she is a family member and not just a dog. Holly goes with Shelly and the family to their coastal house, she swims in the sea, and she has a wonderful life. I would never send Gracie to anyone if I didn't know she would be going to a fantastic home. Let me speak to Shelly for you.'

Mom thanked Cooper but declined his offer of Shelly that night, saying she needed to think things through. She was now undecided on whether to wait out the year or take up Cooper's offer of phoning Shelly. Cooper understood and simply said 'Sweetie it's not fair and I honestly feel your pain. Take all the time you need. All I am doing is offering a life line in case you need it. Stay strong and remember, everything happens for a reason.'

Gracie and I were heart broken. I was trying really hard to understand everything I had heard and so was Gracie. I went to my toy box and pulled out our tug of war rope to play with her, but she was not interested. Now I had Sunny Banana and Gracie who were utterly miserable and nothing I did or said could cheer them up. All I said to Gracie was maybe my Mom would make a plan. She always did. I was sure she would come up with something that would change things.

It wasn't long after that and Steve arrived. It was so fantastic seeing Steve again. It had been over a year. He had lost a lot of weight, but aside from that, he seemed to be doing well. I remember the one evening picking up a scent from Steve that was a little worrying. I made a bit of a fuss around his leg and in the end he understood what I was doing and took his jeans off to show me his leg.

That was not good. He had a cut that started by his groin and it went all the way down his leg to his ankle bone. It was raw and looked very sore to me. So that is what I had been smelling. When Mom saw it, she was shocked I remember her saying 'Dear God in heaven! Steve they have butchered you! Why the hell did they take the artery from your leg? Why didn't they use an artery from your chest or your arm? That looks incredibly painful. Shame man.'

Steve didn't have the answer to that question. All he said was 'perhaps having a quadruple bi-pass along with a valve replacement, they needed something a bit longer to work with. Who knows? It is painful but it's healing. I am going to go for some physio on this leg while I am here and to have a swim in the ocean. Maybe that will help it to heal a bit quicker. I feel a lot better all-round though. But it's still going to be at least a year before I am allowed back on the tennis court according to my surgeon.'

Gracie had an instant fan in Steve and the feeling was mutual. He gushed all over Gracie and then when Mom told him her story about the vet, he is was in tears. He was such a good soul our Steve. He really was in bits once Mom had finished but also said to Mom that he didn't think she had much choice other than to take up Coopers offer. At least she would know, that Gracie is with good people and will be looked after and taken care of until she dies. Steve didn't think it was a good idea to hang around for another year.

Once Steve had settled into his room, I began barking. 'He wants to introduce you to Sunny Banana' said Mom who went on to explain about my and Gracies races against Sunny.

'Common Fin and Gracie, take me to meet Sunny Banana.' Said Steve while doing up his shoe laces. Maybe this would help to cheer up Gracie too. So I was wagging my body, barking and very excited. Mom handed Steve the remote for the electric gate, some apples and a carrot and while laughing said 'Follow Fin and Gracie. See you when you get back'

So Gracie and I took Steve to Sunny Banana who was in a better mood and not feeling so depressed. She was especially happy for the apples and carrot and the three of us prepared for our race. Gracie and I were barking, Sunny Banana was rearing up on her back legs and that's when I said 'Common ol girl, let's see what you got in you today. Last one to the end of the fence is a Rooster!' and we were off.

Sunny Banana was the Rooster that day. Actually if memory serves me correct, I am sure I beat Gracie that day. Steve was watching and I couldn't have a girl beat me in front of him. Besides, racing against Gracie, I had become very fit. Yes I am sure I beat her that day.

When Steve got back to our house he was still laughing when Mom opened the door. He told her he had the best time and it was brilliant to see the friendship between the three of us. It was something he said he would never forget in his life and he was going again tomorrow because the whole experience had been healing.

So every day while Mom was at work, Steve, Gracie and I would visit Sunny Banana and Steve would take her all sorts of delicious treats which she loved. His visits managed to bring her right out of her depression. In fact, for that month, she forgot all about me returning to the UK and we hadn't gotten around to telling her the bad news regarding Gracie.

In the evenings, we would eat dinner together and Steve would tell Mom about his day. The therapy he was going to, along with the visit he had to the boys and any other newsy bits he had to share. I think we all felt safer with having Steve in the house. Not that he would have been able to do much, but it just felt safer somehow.

Mom and Steve used to talk about the crime in South Africa. There were so many poor people of all race and ethnic backgrounds who lived way below the bread line. To be honest their only way to survive was to do crime. As sad as it was, it had become difficult for the honest working person or family to live with. It was affecting people of all colour, creed and race.

I remember Bongani, an African friend of Moms that we used to meet up with at the Flea Market every other Sunday telling her that she was terrified. Her house had been broken into so many times and she used to refer to these people as 'Inkathazo' which is a Zulu word for trouble or a pest. She had family members who had been killed just for the shirt on their back.

Akasha, an Indian woman I had met when going to work with Mom and who I liked very much, had similar stories to share. It seemed to me that no one escaped the 'Inkathazo' No matter how kind you were, or how much security you had to protect your home and family, Inkathazo, would find its way to you and these 'pests' came in all colours, shapes and sizes. All lives were in danger on a daily basis. Poverty was married to crime and getting worse by the hour.

Yes I remember those conversations well. Sometimes the three of them would arrange to meet at the Shongweni Hotel, Gracie and I would lie at Moms feet while her, Bongani and Akasha would natter away for hours over a drink and lunch. Both of them told Mom she was crazy to stay. If they had a choice of staying or returning to the UK, they would have been on a plane already.

Gracie used to lie there listening and would say to me 'Finley, I agree with Moms friends. I will miss you terribly and never forget our time together and I will miss Mom so much, but she cannot stay here just for my benefit. I am sure that this Shelly family are good people. If it is Cooper's niece, then I am sure I will be happy. I will never forget this wonderful family I came into and the happiness it brought me, but I have come to realise that sometimes in life, some things are just not meant to be'

I would tell Gracie to stop talking nonsense. I didn't want to hear it. Mom would make a plan and we would be together forever. She would just smile, close eyes and pretend to be asleep all the while listening to the conversation.

The time came for Steve to fly back to England. The evening before he flew out, Bongani, Akasha, Steve and Mom, had a dinner and a few drinks. Hugs were exchanged, kisses dished out, and tearful goodbyes were exchanged. Everyone promising to meet up in future and to stay in touch.

Following morning before Steve left in his hired car for the airport, he did a stop at Sunny Banana with Gracie and I. He wanted to give Sunny her fruit and he had bought her some sugar lumps. After that he watched us race against Sunny. Once the races were over, Steve held Sunny Banana's big long face in his hands and through the wire he kissed her nose several times and thanked her for helping to heal his leg. He wished her much happiness and then said 'Common Fin and Gracie, it's time for me to say goodbye to your Mom and head to the airport.'

It was a very tearful day. Mom, Steve, Gracie and myself were crying. Mom was thanking him for everything he had done for us while he was there. She wished him a safe flight home and Steve promised to report in weekly regarding his healing process and Mom promised to keep him posted on her return plans.

Just before he climbed in the car he called Gracie and I over 'Gracie, it has been such a pleasure to get to know you. I am beyond heart sore that I may never see your beautiful little face again. It breaks my heart at the thought this may be the last time. Whatever happens with your life Gracie, I wish you a life time of happiness and love. I will never ever forget you. Stay the wonderful, beautiful, brave and loyal girl that you are and I want to thank you both, for helping me to heal and for all the fun and laughter over this past month.

Finley my boy, Go easy on Sunny Banana. You need to let her win a few races. That will cheer her up no end. Remind your Mother where I put the sugar lumps. I know you love them too, but they for Sunny Banana! Until we meet again, look after your Mother for me. Protect her and keep her safe please.'

With that said, he held both Gracie and I and we both got loads of hooter kisses and bear hugs. Then he climbed into the car, wound the window down, waved, tooted the horn and up through the electric gate and along the long driveway he disappeared. Mom was crying and Gracie and I were howling like Wolves. We were all so very sad to see our friend leave.

A couple of days after Steve had left, I remember it was the 2nd December when Mom's future was taken out of her hands. She told us later that fate had intervened. We listened to her conversation to Nan on the telephone 'Mom, you not going to believe this. My boss phoned me today and said 'Danny, you have done an amazing job in Durban and we very happy with you. I know you settled and you don't want to leave South Africa, but I need you back in the UK office. How soon do you think you can wrap up things on this side and get back to England?' I was so shocked that it took me a few seconds to gather myself. Keeping Fin and Gracie in mind and needing to wait another two months for the Serology test to be returned, I told him I would need exactly that, two months. He then says to me, 'sorry, I can't give you that long. You have six week. I want you back in the UK and in the office by the 12th January.' Are you bloody kidding me? I have a fully furnished home, and two dogs to sort out and he gives me six wecks? What do I do about Gracie? It leaves me no time to sort her out. I am literally paining in my chest. I was considering staying until she was ready and now if I don't take his offer, I am unemployed and stuck here.'

It felt like our world was spinning out of control. Mom was in a flat panic. She would need to sell up her house hold contents, pack her previous 27 boxes which had all been opened and the contents of which were now in the house, still go into work every day and she needed to sort out myself and Gracie.

In the middle of all of this, she got a phone call from my Nan one evening, saying she had a heart attack and was due to go into hospital for a couple of stents in two weeks' time. My Nan was very scared of dying and didn't think she would make it. She had bccn ill for so long now and like Steve, she was spraying that stuff under her tongue to open her arteries. Nan has had heart problems for years now. She was sure she would never see us again and was very emotional and tearful.

That of course sent Mom into another blind panic. So she phoned her boss, explained what was going on, asked him to please extend the 12th of January to which he replied 'no' but he did agree to give her leave to fly out and spend a few days with my Nan. Which was very kind of him, but given Mom still had to hold her job every day and pack up an entire house on her own, it now only left her with five weeks in which to do all this.

Everything was happening so quickly and things changed radically on a daily basis. Next time we looked up, Gracie and I were in kennels and Mom had said 'I will be 5 minutes Finley and Grace. I have to go and see Nan and make sure she is comfortable and everything is in order for her op. Behave yourselves and no biting!'

We were staying in the kennels that Gracie had come from so Gracie new Diane well and as a result, we were given free rein. In fact we were not kennelled at all. We were allowed to stay in Diane's house, and we ate dinner with her other dogs every night and during the day we ran around and played with everyone.

It was a fun week and we actually enjoyed ourselves. The week flew by and next time we opened our eyes, Mom was back and we were in the car heading back home. She told us on the drive home that Nan was very ill and we all needed to pray that she made it through this next op.

I prayed so hard that night to Anubis that my Nana would be OK. I had missed her so much and was really very unhappy that something may happen to her. I was sure that Anubis would watch over her and I know Mom was praying to God too. So with both our prayers, I was sure Nana would be fine.

With fate taking everything out of Moms hand, along with that was Gracie. Mom now had no choice, but to accept Shelly's kind offer of giving Gracie a forever home. Gracie had been correct when she said 'somethings in life are just not meant to be' as sad as that made me, I understood. The dream of Gracie and I being together forever, was over and I couldn't blame my Mom and neither could Grace.

The phone calls were made, and the collection date set for Shelly to pick up Gracie. We were to all meet at a house that the boys had in Hillcrest where they stored all their antiques for the shop. Shelly would collect Gracie from there, and she would go on their yearly trip to the coast with Shelly's other Border Collie, Holly and the rest of the family.

Talking about that day breaks my heart. I knew Gracie was going to a good home the minute I smelt Shelly, but the painful memories remain with me all the same.

Mom, Gracie and I were wracked in pain. There was so much crying and hysteria. Cooper was trying desperately hard to calm my Mom down and kept saying to her 'Sweetie please, Gracie is taking terrible strain with your crying. You have to be strong for her sake. Shelly will give Grace a wonderful life. You have to pull yourself together please.'

It was a horrible day. Gracie and I had more or less said our goodbyes the night before after Mom had cried herself to sleep over Grace. We knew we wouldn't get the chance to say the things we needed to the following day. So her and I did a lot of talking, crying, thanking each other for the joy we had shared and promising to pray to Anubis for a future for both of us filled with happiness and barking.

I wished Gracie all the love in the world and promised to say her goodbyes to Sunny Banana. Gracie said she will never forget us as long as she lives. It was the happiest few months of her entire four years of being alive. The memories she would cherish for her remaining years.

Eventually Mom held Gracie, and while she was sobbing she thanked Gracie for being such a wonderful girl. For bringing so much joy into our lives. She also apologized to Grace for not being in position to take her with us back to England and asked Grace to please forgive her for the pain she had caused her little heart, by having to give her to Shelly.

My Mom was clinging to Gracie for dear life and Gracie was licking the tears as they fell from my Moms face. She turned around and said to me, 'Finley, I am going to walk away now. I am going to go over to Shelly and her family and jump in the car. My heart is breaking and if I don't do this, the pain we all feeling won't end. There are no goodbyes Finley. Distance doesn't change that. I will carry you and Mom in my heart forever. I love you Finley. Thank you for being in my life and please always look after Mom. She is going to need you when I leave. Stay calm and protect her. Don't forget to tell Sunny Banana I say goodbye and tell her she runs like a mountain chicken but I shall miss her and pray to Anubis for her wellbeing. Goodbye Finley.'

She gave Moms face a few more licks, walked backwards just staring at mom. 'I love you Gracie' Mom was sobbing and although Mom couldn't understand Gracie, I could hear Grace saying 'I love you too Mom, please don't cry anymore. I am going to be fine. We will meet again one day if not in this life, in our next' Then she turned around and ran towards Shelly and the open door to the back seat of her people carrier van.

Mom was in a terrible state. She mumbled something to Cooper, thanked Shelly very much and begged Shelly to look after Gracie and give her a happy home and then we both got in the car and drove off. She didn't want to watch Grace driving away.

It was one of the worst days and I felt such pain in my heart. I was struggling to breathe the pain was so severe. What I had suffered at the hands of Adam, was nothing compared to the emotional pain and anguish I felt that day. It was back to Mom and I and she was going to need me. We had a lot to do back at the house and I needed to pull myself together because I had a race against Sunny Banana and would have to go through all this upset again tomorrow when relaying Gracie's message.

We got home and Mom was still not right. She kept bursting into a flood of tears. I would go up to her and rest my head on her lap showing her, I understood and it was OK to be sad. This went on the whole day. She would pack a box, then cry her eyes out. Then pack another box, and more crying. If she found anything that Grace had played with, a fresh load of tears. She lost a lot of water out her eyes for the next few days.

To the point that I even had to explain to the Shepherds what was going on because they had heard all the sobbing. As for Sunny Banana, well, she took it rather badly too. She was neighing and very sad that she would never see Grace again and that she was losing her two best friends ever.

Gee things were so sad all round. A little while back we had been so excited to return to England and now, every box was being sealed with Moms snot and tears. She did end up taking leave because there was simply not enough time to pack and do her job.

Lala and Aunty Ivy were very sad that we were returning to England, but at the same time Lala said 'Danny, you doing the right thing.' The boys came around often to help out. They collected all the furniture Mom had bought from them, resold it in their shop and gave Mom back a lot of money which was great.

Austin also sat Mom down at one point. My Mom was miserable and was questioning what life was all about. She was suffering from a bit of depression and wondered where her life was now going. Although she was happy being on her own, she told Austin she wished she could meet a decent man to share her life with.

Austin said to Mom 'Danny, you need to create a vortex. See in your mind's eye a swirl of energy above your head. That vortex is your link to God. You must be very specific about what you want, and don't ask for anything less than you deserve. See the man you would like to share your life with. See every detail. Picture your perfect life, future and happiness. That picture, you put into your vortex, handing it over to God. When you have finished with all the details of the life you want, you say, it is done. God never lets us down. Be careful what you wish for because you will get it. Make sure you are specific and it will be given to you, of that I guarantee you'

So every day, when we went for our walk, and while I was racing against Sunny Banana, Mom was working on her vortex creating a future for us that I had no idea of.

Over the last three weeks of December, our life was manic. Mom had advertised her whole home online and there were hundreds of people in and out. Money changing hands, change given, carrier bags pulled out from boots of cars. It was crazy. Some of the stuff she had wanted to keep and hadn't got around to boxing yet, found it's way in people's boots.

Bongani bought all Moms shoes. Steve had shipped with the Moroccan lamps about ten pairs of shoes for Mom and they were all the wrong size. So she still had them in boxes. They fitted Bongani perfectly. Her and Mom fought for ages over the money. Mom said 'For God sake you my friend. Take the damn shoes as a gift' and Bongani would say 'Listen hear sister, you are going to need every cent on the other side. These are still in their boxes and I refuse to pay nothing. It doesn't work like that in our culture.'

I lost interest in that argument so I don't know whether Bongani paid or not. I went off to make sure the house was safe because there were so many people wondering around. I left Mom and Bongani to their silly argument about who was paying for what, when and how.

Finally after a few days, it was all over. The house was empty of everything that needed to be sold. The fridge and the washing machine were the last things to go. The lady who bought those from Mom said 'Danny, let me know when your last day here is and I will come and collect that from you. I don't want to leave you without a fridge and washing machine.'

Mom said that was very kind of her. So at least we could keep our food fresh right up to the last minute.

The last box was finally sealed 'Dear God that has been exhausting. Well Fin, we are now on our way.' Once her work had come and collected all 27 boxes to be shipped back to England, she sat back on the floor with a glass of wine and took a big sigh of relief.

It had been hectic and all this time, she didn't miss one walk in the evening. Her knee was swollen because her cartilage was playing up. She had somehow hurt it with the moving and packing. The doctor wanted to operate but she refused. Instead she chose to hobble along with a walking stick. I raced against Sunny Banana until my last day. I kept that old girl as fit and happy as I could.

Then disaster struck. As it always did. The weekend before we flew out, we went over to the boy's farm. Me being my usual self, and not being allowed to chase Rooster or his harem, decided to spend my weekend fishing in the pond. Something Cooper had put in the pond water gave me an allergy.

I was meant to be flying out the following Wednesday. Mom would fly out a day later to make sure I had arrived in England safe and sound. She didn't want to risk flying out before I had left, in case for some reason things went wrong.

On the Sunday when we were driving back from Cooper and Austin, I was itching all over and scratching my skin raw. Obviously she noticed because I was on the back seat of the car. When we got home she asked me to lie down so she could check me over. 'Shit Finley! What the hell has gone wrong now? Look at this rash you have. It's an allergic reaction to something. You going to need the Vet. Dammit man, you and that bloody pond!'

So we were no sooner out the car and we were back in the car and off to the emergency Vet. Mom said to the Vet 'Doc, Finley is flying out in three days' time for England. He gets checked by the state Vet in Durban, again in Johannesburg and then London Heathrow. They will not accept him for flight with a rash this bad. Please, I am desperate. Can you fix him in, well, two and a half days?'

'Danny, Finley has an allergy. It's going to take a minimum of three to four days for the rash to calm down. I have prescribed him a ten day course of tablets. I will write a letter for you to give the State Vet. Hopefully they will continue his medication and he will not be showing any signs on arrival in England'

Boy was I in trouble. My Mother was furious with me 'Fuck it Finley. Right at the bloody end of this and with three days to go before you fly, you have to swim for two whole days in that bloody pond and now look! How the hell are we going to clear this up? Your flight is booked and paid for as is mine. You miss this flight and we both sailing up shit creek without a paddle. I am so angry with you.'

Mom gave me a double dose to begin with which wasn't what she was meant to do, but she said desperate times call for desperate measures. So down my throat the double dose went followed by two further tablets that day. Next day, she was checking my rash and there was a slight improvement. On the Monday it was a round of goodbyes for me. Mom took me to the boys first, and I got loads of hugs and fuss from them. I was going to miss them very much. They promised to keep my pond with little fish in for when I came back. Austin even said, next time I come he may have some guinea fowl for me to chase.

Then we visited Lala. I was sad to say goodbye to Lala. She gave me a big hug too and wished me a safe flight. After that, it was back home because Mom said I had to rest.

Day two, was three more tablets and loads of rest. Wednesday, the morning of day three the rash was still there but not as clearly visible at it had been. It was now time for Mom to take me to the airport. But before we left, Mom knew I had to have one more race against Sunny Banana and say goodbye.

That was very sad. Sunny Banana was waiting for me. We decided not to race that day. Sunny Banana and I simply walked the distance we would normally race and we were saying our goodbyes to each other. I couldn't thank Sunny Banana enough for being my dear friend. She felt the same and said she will think of me every day for the rest of her life. Sunny Banana wished she was coming with us. It was a sad goodbye. I put my hooter through the wire and licked her nose with affection. She neighed and reared on her back legs one last time for me and it was time to go.

We got home, Mom grabbed her keys, opened the boot and I jumped in. Everything was a last for both of us. Last time at Lala's house. Last time I would see Sunny Banana. Last time I would travel in this boot and probably the last time I would ever set paw on South African soil again. I was mentally saying my goodbyes to everything around as we drove down our long driveway.

I barked a goodbye to the three German Shepherds who barked back, wishing me the best of luck for the future.

On the way to the airport Mom spoke to me through the review mirror.

'Finley, I am not putting that letter for the State Vet in your travel file. It will draw unnecessary attention to you. There is no way in hell that they going to continue your meds when you meant to be fit and healthy for flight. So I am begging you, please my boy, as tempted as you get, do not scratch in front of anyone. It's imperative you get on that flight for England. Once you alone, if you need to scratch, by all means scratch, but please, please, no scratching while they checking you out and by God's grace, the rash will go unnoticed. I will see you in England in three days' time. If the rash is still there, we can get you antibiotics in England. Now don't forget, this time, I will not be picking you up. Once you have cleared through Heathrow you are going straight into quarantine. You will have to stay there for six weeks because that is the time we are short on your rabies serology test. Fin my boy, have a safe flight. Be a good boy for me. No scratching, and definitely no biting!'

I remember looking at her in the review mirror and smiling to myself. I really did love my Mom and boy she could panic for nothing sometimes. Of course I wouldn't scratch in front of anyone. We were going home and I would do nothing to mess this up. I had forgotten about that quarantine malarkey. I wasn't over joyed with that thought, but at least we would be home and I knew she would visit me like she did in the hospital as often as she could.

Once we arrived at the airport, we followed a lady into a terminal and I recognized the wooden box immediately. Then out came that dreaded stinky spray. Urgh! Why do they do that? That stuff stinks. My documents were checked, the Vet gave me a quick once over and declared me fit to fly to Johannesburg. One hurdle done, two more to go.

Mom got down on her knees and whispered in my ear 'Do not forget everything I have told you!' and then in her normal voice 'Finny Foo, I love you. Tomorrow night you will be on the plane for England. I will see you in 5 minutes. Be a good boy for me please.'

There were no tears and no howls. We both knew this was going to be over very quickly and we were both happy to be heading home. So I wagged my tail, gave her a good barking at, and gladly walked into my wooden crate. I heard the lady saying 'Gee he is a well behaved dog. None of them go into the crate that easily. He is a beautiful animal.' Mom just thanked the lady and said, 'it's time for me to go Fin. Remember what I told you. I love you Fruit Loop'

I was so chuffed. Mom smiled, and I was barking 'Bye Mom, have a safe flight on Friday and I love you too'

She was gone and I was alone in the terminal with the lady and some other people that were loading luggage onto the plane. It wasn't long after that and this man came over with a fork lift, picked up the wooden box with me in it and loaded me into the belly of the airplane. Yep, I had done all this before and knew the drill. I was an international traveller for sure. My real Mom would not believe all the adventures I had been on. Let alone all that I had learned about humans, horses, roosters, slippery fish, angry dogs, monkeys, life and emotions.

I slept the whole flight to Johannesburg. It's not a long flight. Maybe an hour and you there. My crate was picked up again by a fork lift and loaded into a vehicle that was waiting for me on the runway. From there I went to a quarantine animal section to be checked over by the Big Vet.

To be fair, once I arrived at the quarantine place and was put in a kennel, I realized I wasn't feeling all that well. Maybe it was that stinky stuff they sprayed in my crate. Maybe it was my rash, maybe it was just the heat, but I felt a bit iffy.

I wasn't as itchy as I had been and was very careful not to let anyone see me scratching. Mind you, Mom did give me my daily three tablets that are meant to be spaced over 24 hours, in the space of 6 hours. Maybe that was it. The Big Vet never arrived that day. So dinner was served in my kennel and it was awful. To this day, I do not know what they tried to feed me, but it was just horrible. That evening I lay thinking about Mom, Gracie and Sunny Banana.

Just before I left Durban, Cooper had sent Mom some photos of Gracie on the beach with Shelly and the family. Mom showed me the photos and Gracie looked happy. There was also a little video of her chasing the kids and bouncing on a trampoline. Both Mom and I cried looking at the pictures and watching the video, and although our hearts were still very sore, we could see, Gracie was having the time of her life and we couldn't ask anymore from God and Anubis.

I remember that last night in Johannesburg was a long one and in many ways lonely. I can't really explain it, but so much had happened in the fifteen months we had been here. I had heard Mom telling Nan 'What we went through in fifteen months, people don't experience in a life time!' The arrival at Owens. Me meeting poor sick little Milo who ended up under the wheel of Owens 4x4. The drama and upset at Adam. Mom and I sleeping with a gun every night. The sjambok I received from Adam still gave me nightmares.

Then Harper's house. The swimming pool, the little cottage, the friend Miles let into Moms house every day while she was at work. The guns being fired at night. The big storm. Then the drive to Lala and everything we had gone through together in Hillcrest. Wow! Mom was right. We had crammed a lifetime into fifteen short months. It all just seemed like a crazy dream. What I was looking forward to was the winter back home, snow ball fights with Mom, and believe it or not, listening to Gordie's History lectures.

Next day, strangely enough, I wasn't itching at all. I think Moms 24 hour dose of antibiotics in the space of 6 hours had chased my rash well away. It was too scared to show its face in case Mom was there with her pill box! So when the Big Vet came to give me a thorough looking over, he saw nothing that should prevent me from flying home. I was issued a clean bill of health, my passport stamped and not long after that, loaded back into my crate with my document folder stapled to the top of the crate. I was on my way home.

I was flying in a really big plane this time. There were a few other dogs and cats being loaded at the same time. I watched them from several crates back. Just before the fork lift picked the crate up, a woman would spray that awful stinky stuff into it. One by one, I could hear the dogs and cats moaning about the awful smell.

Wasn't long and it was my turn to have it all over my small crate and in my fur. I was not impressed. I wondered what the inflight menu held for us on this flight home. Once we were all loaded along with the luggage, the doors were closed and that was us. I knew the next time that door opened, I would be back in England. This time I was on a direct flight. I could hear my Mom in my head wishing me a safe flight. Without a doubt, she would have phoned to make sure I had boarded this plane. So in my thoughts, I told her I was safe, comfortable, I would see her in two days' time and I loved her. I knew she would get my mental message. She always did.

I chatted to a few of the other dogs and cats. They were really very scared and as I had done this before, it was my duty to tell them it was all going to be just fine. For most of them, the final destination was England. A few others were en route to the USA and Canada. One poor cat had something silly like two full days of flying. Poor thing was going to Australia via London. I was glad I wasn't her.

They all had stories to tell. Mostly around the crime and how their families had decided it was not safe to live in South Africa any more. It was sad listening to their tales. Some of them had even experienced the death of an owner who had been shot or stabbed.

As we settled into the flight, our food was brought along and through a hatch on the side of the wooden crate they piled some stuff into a bowl for us to eat. To be fair, I don't know what it was, but it was quite tasty. It tasted a bit like spam to me and I really enjoy that when Mom gives it to me. So I ate some dinner and decided to get some rest in. I left all the other dogs and cats talking about their lives and the hopes for their futures.

I curled up on my blanket and wondered what the next fifteen months would bring us. If all the creations in Moms vortex came true, and that direct link to God that Austin told her she had was true, we were in for a great time! I fell asleep dreaming of chasing squirrels again, swimming in my favourite lake and finding Gordies hidden stash of treats my Nan always gave him. He was a craft boy, hiding his treats from me, but Mom always says 'Finley has the scent of a blood hound' I can find anything, hidden anywhere!

Chapter 9

The flight back to the UK was uneventful. I slept most of the way and when I wasn't sleeping I lay listening to the stories coming from the other flight companions. I was really happy when I realized we had landed at Heathrow. It wouldn't be long and I would be out this crate and breathing good English air back into my lungs.

When the door to the plane opened, I gasped. Wow! We were definitely back home. It was freezing cold. I was actually shivering even with my thick coat. I had left South Africa on 35 degrees and landed in England to zero degrees. It was so, so cold but it felt fantastic to me. Once I got my breath back, it was wonderful. Oh how I had missed this weather.

As usual, those of us whose final destination was England, were all picked up by a forklift and transferred into a waiting van. Because I was going into Quarantine, my journey was a little different. I never went to the holding facility at Heathrow. I was picked up directly by the quarantine carrier who would be looking after me for the next few weeks.

I was the only dog going to this particular quarantine. As the van was driving I was picking up familiar smells. I was sure Mom and I had travelled on this road many times. I couldn't see out the van, but my senses were telling me I had done this journey before. I was in the van for about 45 minutes and then it stopped. The back door opened and a lovely lady was there to greet me.

I was taken out my crate, and walked to the cage that I would be staying in for the next six weeks. I was pleased to be walking. My joints were a bit stiff and my leg was a bit achy.

When I arrived, all ten cages on my block were empty. In the next block there was a poodle called Gigi. She had been in Quarantine for four months already and had another few months to go. Her parents had brought her in illegally in a handbag from Europe and got caught at the airport. So she was doing her time and going through all the different phases that Gracie would have had to go through. Her parents were allowed to visit her, but it had been a long stay for Gigi.

The cage I was in, had a sleeping area where a bed had been put down for me along with a couple of blankets, a bowl of water and it had an enclosed wire area which was mine to walk in. There was a door from the sleeping side to the walking side. Unfortunately because it was so cold, the door to my walking area was only opened for about 30 minutes a day. I personally have no problem with the cold, but I believe not all dogs can handle the cold so for their own health and safety, we all got the same 30 minutes a day to wonder outside into our private space.

I think it was that same afternoon that the Big, BIG Vet came and checked my paperwork, listen to my heart, took my blood, checked my ears, took my temperature, pushed my fur back to check my skin, looked at my teeth, and finally after all that fuss, I heard him say 'You a very good boy for allowing me to check you out like this and you in good health Finley! Welcome home. I am sure your Mom will be visiting you soon.'

And he was gone. I was alone on that particular block with no one to talk to. Well that is not strictly true, there was Gigi, but she was so far away and right at the bottom end of our block of kennels. That made it difficult to talk to her and I had no idea what she even looked like. I suspect she had the same view I did. Nothing. Other than the corridor that the staff would walk down when they came to clean your cage, feed you or fill your bowl up with fresh water. It was also the corridor that visitors arrived down.

I remember thinking my Mom will be so pleased to see her overdose on antibiotics worked and that my rash was gone. I knew by now she must know that I had arrived safe and sound. She would be flying out that same evening because I remember her telling me, 'when you land Finley, I will be on my way to the airport in Durban' Which meant, I will probably see her soon.

Well, the next six weeks thankfully flew by. I made friends with all the staff who even wrote on my chart that hung on the door 'a beautiful mild tempered boy' they all loved me and brought me little treats and gave me extra fuss. I remember the first time my Mom saw that sign on my door, she burst out laughing and said 'Clearly, they have only seen your Dr Jekyll side and have yet to meet Mr Hyde! Mild tempered? Seriously Finley?' she thought it was very funny.

I remember being actually rather offended and turned my face away when she knelt down to kiss me. I was only nippy and aggressive protecting my Mom. I really did not appreciate her comment. My snubbing her, only brought on more laughter. In the end, she said 'Finley I am teasing you. Don't be upset with me. It's just funny to see you being called mild tempered when everyone who knows you, would disagree with that. I don't think there is a bum on two continents that you haven't nipped at some point! But I am super proud of you and well done for being such a good boy while you stay in Quarantine' Now that's better! So we kissed and made up.

'How is your rash Finny Foo? Lie down let me check' she asked. So I lay down and rolled over for to have a look 'Wow! It's gone! Fantastic!' she said while clapping her hands. It was wonderful to see her again. I had missed her, even though it had only been a couple of days.

After she left that first day, I was thinking about this nipping thing. There were bums I had not nipped. OK! Not many, but still. Even a handful counts. Surely! I vowed to work on my nipping and I hoped Mom didn't say anything to the staff because they all thought I was amazing and I enjoyed their company when they did come down my corridor.

She obviously didn't mention my nipping to anyone because nothing changed. Mom would visit me almost every day and the staff still fussed over me. I kept my chompers well away from all their bums! Some days she was held up at meetings and didn't make the visiting hour time slot. On the days she didn't make it, she would leave a message with Betty who worked at the Quarantine place and was the main person who visited me. Betty would come with her cleaning equipment and say 'Finley your Mom won't make it today, but she said to tell you she loves you and will see you tomorrow.' I always enjoyed my messages from Betty.

As much as I enjoyed my messages from Betty, when I heard Mom's car pull up I was always so excited to see her. She used to bring me loads of goodies, and she was given permission to bring one of my balls so her and I would play with the ball in my small outdoor area. Having Mom there also meant I was allowed in my outdoor space for as long as she stayed. I was not restricted to my usual thirty minutes a day.

Shame I remember she was always freezing and so uncomfortable sitting on the cold concrete floor. In the end she used to bring a blanket to sit on. Had a scarf, beanie, gloves, and big thick jacket on. She always sat the full visiting time whether it rained or snowed, she sat outside in my little caged area. After we had played a bit, I would lie with my head on her lap and she would tell me stories of her day and what was going on outside of the quarantine camp.

She arrived one day singing Happy Birthday from far away. I was wagging my body. I didn't know it was my birthday! As you know, I love my birthday. Then I saw her coming down the corridor singing the song all over again 'Happy birthday to you, happy birthday to you, happy birthday dear Finley, happy birthday to you'

I noticed the Lidl packet in her hand. Oh boy I was excited. That could only mean one thing 'mackerel' Woohoo! I had no space to do a victory lap, but I was jumping up and down and running in tight circles on my blankets from happiness. 'Now let's see what I have for you today Fruit Loop. Hmmm….. Ah yes, one packet of mackerel, and oh my gosh! Look what fell into the packet, some liver biscuits, AND some chocolate biscuits!'

Well that was me, in dog heaven. Mom hadn't baked me liver biscuits in ages and they were so good. I feasted while she put her blanket down on the cold floor outside, and got herself comfortable. She had brought a Costa Coffee and we shared the chocolate biscuits.

That is when she told me that we were going to live with my Nan, Gramps and Gordie until we found a house of our own. She also said Gordie was very excited to see me and that he was already finding new hiding places for his stash. That made me bark and wag my body in laughter, did he really think he could get one over me? I had every intention of sniffing out his hidden stash when I got out of here.

Mom was very happy to be back in England and had a very positive attitude which I hadn't seen for ages now. There was no more fear and stress in her energy. She was a different woman. Me? I had gotten so used to quarantine, my daily chats with Betty, Mom visiting and then leaving, that it hadn't dawned on me that I would be leaving soon. Mom had mentioned it on her last visit, but I was terrible with time. One day just blended in with another.

Then one day, a lady from the office that I didn't know that well came and collected me. I wasn't sure where we were going but it was great to be out and on my lead seeing new things other than my cage. I wondered where we were going and my tail abruptly stopped wagging, when I realized I was being led to the wash room for a bath.

Seriously? Why? Why on Earth do I have to have one of those horrible things? I hate bathing! Oh I was so unimpressed. She explained to me 'Finley your Mom is collecting you today. You going home boy. So we getting you cleaned up and smelling fresh for when she arrives.' I knew it! My Mother had to be behind this torture. What is it with my Mom and baths?

After I had been blow dried and brushed, everyone commented on how wonderful I looked and smelt. I didn't give a hoot. I was really fed up and I didn't care how much my coat was shining, how many knots they got out, how much bum fluff they had trimmed or any of that malarkey. I sulked all the way back to my cage which had all the staff laughing and there I waited for the sound of my Moms car. I was going to Nan, Gramps and to find Gordie's hidden stash pot.

As she approached my cage with the lady from the office, she commented 'Oh wow! Look at you! You all clean and fluffy again. Looking good Fin' when she saw my expression she burst out laughing and said to Betty 'He's got the shits with me. He thinks I ordered his Bath! Betty, did I ask you to bath Finley?' asked Mom and Betty replied laughing 'No you didn't. We always bath the dogs on the day they leaving because invariably they don't smell that great after being locked in a cage for weeks or months on end. Finley your Mother had nothing to do with your bath' Betty was laughing so much.

I cocked my head sideways like I usually do and gave my Mom an intense look. Was she telling me the truth or had her, and Betty conspired against me? After studying them both and reading their energies, I concluded she was telling the truth. So I barked, wagged my body and was saying to her 'common less chatting and more walking. I need to get out of here. Common Mom, let's go!' I remember Betty's parting comment after Mom thanked everyone for taking such good care of me 'Danny, Finley is one of a kind. He had us all under his spell and he is certainly the cleverest dog we have ever looked after. I think I speak for everyone, when I say, he will be missed.'

I remember thinking 'Yeah love you too, bye!' I hadn't jumped that quickly into the boot of any of mom's cars in ages. I just wanted out of there. It was enough. I had freedom again. Oh boy was I looking forward to my new life. On the way home Mom asked me 'Fin, do want to stop off for a walk in the woods first?' hell yes! I barked and barked.

It felt like heaven to have mud and grime under my paws again. The ground was freezing cold and in many places, frozen. It felt wonderful. I ran and ran. I played with other dogs, I chased a duck back into the cold half frozen lake just for the hell of it. Squirrels ran from me, Swans gave me a stern warning 'keep walking boy' so I left them alone. It was just fantastic to be out that cage and back in the real world.

When Mom pulled into my Nan's driveway, I was barking from the boot 'Gordie? I'm back! I'm coming for your stashed treats' I saw Gordon run onto the balcony landing at the top of the staircase and I laughed. That staircase had been the cause of a few arguments between us on who had barking rights and when.

Gordon the cheeky chap was laughing and barking back 'Finley! I have hidden them well this time. You won't find them even with your Bloodhound scent. Oh! And I watched a documentary last night on the invasion of the Vikings and all their raids in the 8th Century which I know you will be just dying to listen to!'

Dammit! I had forgotten how annoying Gordon can be with all the TV documentaries he watches with my Nan and Gramps. I was in for days of historical lectures. Urgh, I remember thinking 'Mom take me back to quarantine please. It's bound to be less torture than listening to Gordon bang on and on about the stuff he watches.'

Mom was laughing at the barking between Gordie and I. She had no idea what we were talking about, but she could see we were having fun exchanging information. If she only knew what was facing me with Gordon.

But it was great to see my old friend again. I jumped out the boot and by this time my Nan was on the stairs 'Hello Finley! Welcome home. You looking so good my boy. We missed you very much' I was so happy to see my Nan. I ran up the driveway at full speed, up the stairs and jumped up against my laughing Nan. I was home with the people who meant the most to me.

As it always happens, you think things are going swimmingly well and then BAM! It all changes. I had wondered why I never saw my Mom on her 50th Birthday. Turns out she spent it with Ryan the Narcissist. Of all the people to have spent her birthday with she chose him. Gordie told me she had seen him loads of times while I was in quarantine. She kept that very quiet! Not once did she tell me she was dating that man again.

I was really so angry with her. Why would she put herself through all that again? It made no sense to me at all. Besides where was Steve? I asked Gordie one evening 'Gords, have you seen or heard anything about Steve?' and all he could tell me was 'I did hear your Mom talking about him the other day to my mom and she said something about her and Steve having a fall out back in December. Something about him being so rude to her at the airport and ignoring her attempts to contact him. Then when she arrived back and Ryan got in touch, even though Steve had now reached out to her in the form of a simple waving hand on

Facebook, one, she was angry with him for being such a jerk and two, she was too embarrassed to talk to him because if he found out she was dating Ryan again, she couldn't bare the look on his face or the comments that would follow. So she was keeping Steve away for now. Or something like that'

'Ah yes, you right Gordie. I had forgotten about that. Mom told me about it when she got back from visiting Nan in December before her heart op. Steve has always had two cars. So Mom asked him if she could please use one of them so she had transport for the few days she would be in England. Steve of course said yes, and they arranged to meet at a certain place at Heathrow Airport on the day of her arrival.

Somehow, Mom was waiting in one place and Steve in another. One of them had misunderstood. Steve was very angry that Mom had kept him waiting, and when he found her, he shoved the keys in her hand, told her what floor the car was on, and simply walked away without even a hello or goodbye.

When she had tried to call him to find out what on earth was wrong, he let all her calls go into voice mail. She sent him dozens of messages and not one was replied. So the whole time she was with my Nan she never saw or heard from Steve. The day she was flying back to South Africa, Steve was waiting at the agreed spot, he simply took the keys out her hand and walked off again with no hello, goodbye or explanation.

He hurt my Mom very deeply with his behaviour. She had left a thank you card in the car along with a bottle of his favourite Whisky and flowers. Still she heard nothing from Steve. Yes I remember now. My Mom had no clue what she had done or said to hurt or anger Steve to that extent. So she simply pulled back and decided she was not going to try contacting him anymore.' I explained to Gords.

I hadn't finished so I added 'And so she should be embarrassed about going back to Ryan! I can't believe she is going down that road again. She has been fine for the past three years without him. I am so upset to hear this news' Gordie just replied with 'Fin, it's not your business. These are human things and we probably just don't understand their emotions or feelings very well.'

'Oh what a load of wobblegong! I understand perfectly what is going on here. It's my Mother that doesn't! I have heard people talking and they say it's a low self-esteem. She is being manipulated all over again. She can't possibly allow herself to be cheated on, lied to, devalued and ultimately discarded again. She was so strong once she kicked him out the last time. We were happy and so was she. Why? Why would she go back to all the emotional and mental abuse again? Oh this is such bad news.' I barked out.

Gordon was just staring at me. He really had no idea of what life had been like for both of us under Ryan's influence. How could he? His world was very different from mine. His parents had been together for decades and he was spiffy on History and medical issues. If you have a spot on your bum that needs diagnosis, Gordie is the go to dog for that. But when it came to general life issues, he is tad naïve.

It's difficult to explain really. Gordon and I have different strengths. Gordie has grown up with a very clever Mom and Dad who are both Historians and also my Nan has suffered poor health for many years and Gordon is well up to speed on anything medically based. Which I am not.

I have grown up with my Mom telling me everything. I was her only friend and personal company really. Yes she had my Nan, Jessica, the boys, Lala, Bongani, Akasha, Steve and the others, but it was me who lay at the bottom of her bed at night. It was me who protected her. It was me who watched her many nights when she was with Ryan. Crying with a bottle of red wine and a toilet roll. There was very little, if anything, I didn't know about my Mom.

Patience! I needed to just watch and listen to her conversations to see where this was all going. One thing I did know, was the next time I saw Ryan, I was going to nip his bum. I was no longer a six month old puppy he could push around and bully. If he upsets my Mom he will have me to deal with.

Over the next few weeks, I would hear loads of conversations between my Mom, my Nan and Jessica. From what I could piece together, Mom had given Ryan some kind of ultimatum. He had one year to prove himself and make a commitment and if he didn't, she would pack his bags for him and this time it would be for good.

She also told him in no uncertain terms that if she felt just mildly manipulated, bullied, or emotionally abused, she would not hesitate to send him packing. I heard her telling my Nan one day that she had told Ryan 'You used to tell me that I would be lost without you. I wasn't. Breaking up with you again, will be a small price to pay for my sanity and wellbeing. It's your call. Tow the line or move on'

By all accounts, Ryan was being very nice to my Mom and really putting his best foot forward. My Nan told Mom 'Danny listen to your intuition. You keep ignoring it and coming unstuck. If you get that vague sense of dread, run my girl. You cannot go through all this pain again. I personally cannot see how this leopard will have changed its spots, but it's your life and your mistakes you have to make. All I can do, is give you advice and be there for you when it inevitably goes wrong'

Jessica, Mom's friend said 'Oh Dannydandan…. What can I say to you that I haven't said a thousand times before? From seventeen years of friendship, fourteen of those we have spent talking about Ryan! Our friendship is not defined by who you choose to date and share your life with. Whether I agree with your decisions or not, you are my friend first and foremost.

Nothing would ever come in the way of my love for you. However, I will say this, Ryan will go to just about any length to get you back. Quite obviously he has exhausted his supply of victims and is going through a dry spell! In my opinion, you mistaking his trickery for genuine remorse. I don't for a minute believe that there is a genuine desire from Ryan to make this relationship work. Personally, I feel he is behaving like a praying mantis.

He will lure you in with calculated appeal and wait for a weak moment to make his move. His timing will be perfect as usual, and the first sign of vulnerability and you done for. You know and I know, this is all about sex for Ryan. Whether you care to admit that to yourself or not, it's the truth. But as usual, your Mother and I will be around to pick up all the pieces. What a crying shame you are so strong in all areas of your life and so utterly weak when it comes to this prick.'

Mom used to say, there is no bridal that fits Jessica's mouth. She shoots from the hip. Always has and always will. If you not strong enough to hear the truth, for god sake don't ask Jessica for advice!

So it's not like my Mom wasn't warned or she didn't know who she was getting involved with. I vowed that day to find her a good man. When we went out on our walks, I would see what potential partners there were and maybe try and get the two to meet. I had to do something. I couldn't help wandering what had happened to that vortex and link to God that she posted her wish list through. Clearly God was on holiday and had not got around to opening his vortex Mail yet.

Less than two months after arriving at my Nan, my Mom came home and said 'Mom I have found a lovely two bed house to rent. I have passed the checks. Ryan helped me with the deposit and Finley and I will move out in two weeks' time. Actually it's just around the corner from Layla which will be nice. Finley will get to play with Willow again'

Nan was very happy for Mom but in equal measures, she was sad we were moving out so soon. She loved us living there but Mom wanted more space and also she was under pressure from her boss to pick up her twenty seven boxes that were sitting taking up space in the warehouse. There was nowhere for her to load the boxes at my Nan and so with that pressure mounting, she decided to look for a home for us.

I wasn't impressed Ryan was helping with the deposit. That would just give him a say in our lives, but what could we do. At least I guess we had a new home to go to. That afternoon, Mom drove my Nan, Gordie and myself to look at our new home. Urgh, it looked so ugly from the outside. I didn't dislike the house, but it wasn't the farm we had left behind to move to Durban that's for sure! At least I had a small garden and there were loads of lovely walks we could go on. Also there were two big rugby pitches to run on.

I saw loads of dogs that day and they were all so friendly. So on that score, I was excited. All the dogs were saying hello to me and asking me if I wanted to come and play ball with them. I had to decline and explain to them that we hadn't moved in yet, but soon I would be joining them. That was the day I met Eddie the Labrador, Vinnie the Red Setter and Shadow the Husky.

Now I was excited to move. I had made a few friends within minutes and I was going to love living here. I didn't even notice how ugly the house was anymore. In fact, I began to think it was really cool. Gordie was telling me how lucky I am to be moving here and to have made friends already. He said he was going to really enjoy visiting with my Nan. He couldn't wait to race me across the rugby field and we were betting our treats on who would win.

Obviously me! Gordie was having none of it. His challenge was 'Finley, you a lump! You big and heavy. Me? I am just built for speed. I will wipe those smiling whiskers right off your Aussie baggy chops. If you win, which you won't, I will give you my pig's ear. If I win, which I will, I want your tripe stick. Do we have a deal?'

'Yes you have a deal. But when I win, which I will, I also want along with your pig's ear, that menthol dental stick that I found hidden under Nans carpet in her bedroom which believe it or not, I didn't take!' I replied with my laughing bark which grew even louder when I saw Gordie reaction on mentioning his 'well hidden' stash. Once the shock of his hidden dental stick had worn off and he had made it very clear that I was not to eat his dental stick, we both agreed, and did a little victory lap of excitement.

The future race would be held the next time Gordie visited and once Mom and I had moved in and settled. I hoped that would be soon. I was dying to put Gordon in his place once and for all. I was so sure that my months of practice against Sunny Banana and Gracie would make me much faster than Gordie who in my opinion had become a small, fat cocktail sausage in the fifteen months that I had been away.

I remember the challenges between Gordon and I grew bigger over the two weeks before we moved out. We were betting balls, tug of war ropes, fluffy toys, treats, and old lamb bones. We were both such show offs in our own right and neither of us wanted to appear weak, so we just bigged ourselves up. Looking back it was really very funny.

We didn't actually have that much to pack because Mom had packed everything into our returning boxes and only kept the essentials out. A few days before she was due to pick up the keys she came home with bad news. She was telling my Nan 'Mom, I have lost my job. John says that he is very sorry, but that the USA lane of traffic I was handling is not going well. The office in the States is doing badly, and there is not enough business coming in to cover my salary. He was very apologetic, but it ended with him saying 'well at least you back in England and this didn't happen to you in South Africa' which I am thankful for. He is quite right. It would have been an absolute disaster if this had happed back in Durban. The man was instrumental in bringing me back to the UK and for that, I should be grateful. I am just so worried. The Logistics market is in a mess. Where on Earth am I going to find a job? I have just signed for this house and we moving in a few days' time. God Mom, it never rains but it pours. Sometimes, I truly despair. Will I ever find my feet? It always seems that I take a few steps forward and then get knocked back. What next?'

My Nan was very worried about my Mom. Not only because she was walking down a road of disaster by rekindling her relationship with Ryan, but now, she had no job. She asked my Mom if there was any way she could cancel the house and Mom said no. Everything is signed and paid for. There was no going back now. All my Nan could really do was tell Mom to stay positive. Everything would come right. Life has a way of just sorting itself out.

Later that night she phoned Austin and Cooper. They were both very sad to hear that the wheels had fallen off yet again. Austin asked Mom 'Danny, are you still using your vortex?' and Mom told him she was. Every day she took me for a walk she was posting emails to God through the vortex. Which surprised me because I had not heard her talking out loud to her vortex for ages.

Austin went on to say 'Danny, this is life. Despite our best intentions, things can, will, and do, go wrong. It's how we deal with it when it happens that matters. Right now, you feeling anxious and dejected, but you cannot dwell on those emotions. Do not feed those negative thoughts.

Please listen to me. No matter what your circumstances are and no matter how bad you think they are, you have the power to change those energies. You can use the energies around you in a positive or negative way. Either way Sweetheart, the decisions you make today will determine your future. You need to have a calmer attitude and accept these changes with grace.

There is a reason this is happening and you need to stay alert to see why. If you fall into that pity party for one, you will miss the opportunity that will present itself. Nothing in our life is coincidental. Be grateful for your new home, the support you getting, the financial help from Ryan. He has come back into your life for a reason, and this may very well be that reason. By being grateful even for your job loss, it gives you a much wider perspective and you will feel less overwhelmed. Have faith. I keep telling you. Faith! The Universe has your back. It's not punishing you, it's simply moving you in the direction it needs you to go.

If you are doing your vortex daily, in order to give you the future you need, certain things may have to go, or be changed. So embrace this job loss and know, that God has a reason for doing this. In order to create way for the new, we have to move out the old. Stay calm, stay clear and stay confident. You will see Sweetheart, it will all work out the way it's meant to.'

After that conversation with the boys, Mom's spirits picked up. She told my Nan she felt better and that Austin was right. Now was not a time to feel sorry for herself. If she couldn't find a job back in the Industry, then she would find something else to keep the wolf from the door. Or as she said to Nan in our case, it's keeping the wolf off our sofa!

When she told Jessica what had happened, Jessica was her usual unbridled self 'Danny, this Industry is dominated by testosterone and over inflated egos. What this company has done to you is disgusting and utterly shameful. But it is what it is and moaning about it won't change a thing. The facts are you a woman and fifty. You are going to struggle to find a new job. They looking for younger, more exciting blood. Now is your chance to stay out. If

I were you, I would not be going back. I can count on one hand after thirty odd years in this rat pack, the amount of woman over fifty still employed in the industry. Look at it as they have done you a favour. Let Ryan help you out, God knows he owes you at least that much, and take your time to find something else'

From that day and until we moved, she kept her positive attitude. She accepted the small pay off from her boss with grace. She bought her company car because her boss was going to auction it as he would not be replacing Mom. So she at least had wheels, and she paid with what little money she had left, a couple of months insurance up front.

We visited a lot of charity stores in the last days because we had 27 boxes of stuff and no furniture. She found a great Charity store that sold furniture and she bought a sofa for £85, a double bed for £90, a work desk for £35, a kitchen table and chairs for £25 and a washing machine for £85. The new house came with curtains and although a little weather beaten, they would do just fine until we had money to replace them.

The day Mom went to pick up the keys and do her check in she was told it was part of an Army Division. She was telling my Nan 'it was quite interesting really. The agent said where we moving was a British Army Garrison and in 2015 most of the military vacated and a large part of the base was opened up for development and housing. The house Fin and I are moving into was last lived in ten years ago! There are still active military personal that live on the Estate but the vast majority of the houses are now rented by the public.'

Chapter 10

It was the easiest move Mom and I had done together. Mom had arranged that pretty much everything arrived either on the very day we moved in or the following day. So she left me with Nan and Gordie. The car was packed with stuff that she had taken with her as luggage from South Africa, and other bits and pieces she had bought from The Range to again make our new house feel more like a home.

At the new house she met the van driver from the Charity Store and they helped her with her bed, the sofa, desk, kitchen table and a washing machine. Once that was all sorted, she came back to fetch me. We said our goodbyes to Nan and Gordie and Mom said she would see Nan once we had settled in.

I was surprised when I arrived at our new house because Mom had done a lot of work in the hours she had been away. The house was actually very nice inside and I knew that once she opened her 27 boxes and her carpets, ornaments, photos and other bits and pieces all got to feel fresh air again, the house would take shape.

The garden was very small. The total outdoor space was 6m x 7m. In the middle of the concrete was a patch of lawn 3.5m x 4m and it had grown waist high over the years. Mom had taken my Nans strimmer and that afternoon she cut it all down. She said it desperately needed a small lawn mower but that would have to wait. Maybe she could find one at the Charity Store. I at least, had somewhere to wee and poo if and when I needed to.

That first day, other than cutting the lawn and packing her things in the cupboard, there wasn't much else to do. The boxes were meant to be arriving the following day and that was when all the hard work would begin. So we went for a walk to investigate. On the rugby field, I spotted Eddie the Labrador and Vinnie the Red Setter.

I ran over to play with them and Mom introduced herself to their owners. They all stood chatting, and we chased tennis balls for ages. We hadn't been there long and Maisey the Border Collie arrived with her owner Dylan. I liked Dylan straight away. I got a good smell from him but he was not the one for my Mother. I could sense that. He liked her and she liked him, but that is where it ended. My Mother had the same scent towards Dylan that she did towards Steve, so I knew it was a no go for her. It did however, give me hope that maybe, just maybe, there was someone else out there.

That first night was actually pleasant. The outside area was very private and you couldn't really see into the back yard unless you stood on a box and peered through the crisscross fencing. It had a high wall and then wooden crisscross fencing on top. So Mom kept the door open and she sat outside on a blanket with a glass of wine and I lay next to her.

Following day was hectic. All twenty seven boxes arrived and there were boxes everywhere. They were delivered on these huge pallets and ceremoniously dumped outside of the back yard gate. Mom had her work cut out for her that's for sure. It was taking up space on the common walk way and she had to work quickly to get those boxes taken off the huge pallets and carried one by one into our garden area. From there she would take one at a time into the house.

My Nan, Jessica and the boys were phoning to see how she was getting on and she told them all 'Please just let me finish and I will call you back. I am up to my back teeth in bloody boxes. They big boxes and bloody heavy. I cannot believe I carry around all this crap. God's truth! I am such a hoarder. Who moves rocks around with them? They stones I have picked up on my travels. Other people buy T-shirt's, post cards or gift novelties, me? I take stones home. I seriously need my head read'

I was laughing to myself. The boxes had been in the warehouse for a few months now and they were filthy. She had black soot all over her face. I just lay there watching her. I couldn't really help and watching her mood gradually change colour, it was best I kept out of her way.

She eventually came across my old toy box and in there I found an old marrow bone from South Africa, so I lay chewing on that, and wondering how Gracie and Sunny Banana were. I still missed them so much. Ryan phoned her during that day and said he would be around over the weekend. He asked her if she needed anything and she told him we were fine. She also said that he was in for a shock when he sees me because I have grown up to be a magnificent animal and I am extremely handsome.

Well, twenty two of the boxes were opened that day and unpacked. The other five boxes were paper work, photo albums, old charges, cell phones that belonged in the dark ages, electronic connections that connected to nothing, loads of chargers and wiry things which she had no clue what they did or were for. In the end she said 'to hell with this' closed the lids on the boxes and shoved them all under the staircase in the storage cupboard.

That whole day she was busy. It literally took her forever. In the end though it looked comfortable. Once she had put her carpets out, hung some paintings, put clean matching linen on the bed, decorated the bathroom, sorted the kitchen out, and turned her spare room into an office it looked like we had lived there for ages.

As Mom always says 'We have the basics to make a home comfortable and that was all we needed.' She would buy additional bits and pieces as and when. Ryan had phoned and said all the kitchen stuff they had when they lived together almost four years ago now, was still packed in boxes and in his attic. He would bring them all over on the weekend because he had no use for them.

That kitchen stuff I can remember being the cause of a big fight when Ryan was leaving last time with his cats. Everything Mom and Ryan had, they bought together. Ryan however was adamant that he had paid for the kitchen stuff and therefore it was not to be split. After all these years, it was making its way back to our kitchen. Humans are so strange. Even though I had come to understand them so well, they still managed to surprise me.

That first weekend of Ryan arriving was relatively pain free aside from when he followed Mom to bed and they closed the bedroom door. I cried my heart out. I was howling like a wolf outside the closed door. To the point that Ryan yanked the door open and said to Mom 'This is ridiculous. I can't have sex with this dog carrying on like this!'

I couldn't help it. I was in agony. I felt a deep sadness because Mom was opening herself up to all this pain again. The whole experience for me was overwhelming. Although he was very nice to Mom and tolerant of me, didn't change the fact that his smell had not changed. There was far more to Ryan than what my Mom was seeing. The distrust I felt I couldn't shake off.

Over the weekend the boxes Ryan brought with him were opened and all the old kitchen stuff came out. We now had a dinner service, pots, pans, knives, forks, you name it, and we had it. Our kitchen was fully stocked and we needed nothing more.

I was very happy when Sunday morning came and Ryan was saying 'Right that's me! I am heading home. I think you now have everything you need. If you need any money let me know and I will transfer some funds into your account. You really need to sort this dog out. If I am going to be coming on weekends, we can't have a repeat of all the howling of this weekend. He needs discipline and boundaries.'

He gave Mom a brief, insincere hug and ruffled my hair before turning to leave through the front door. I don't know what overcame me that day, but as he turned his back on us, I lunged for him and sunk my teeth into his bum.

Ryan was not impressed. He grabbed me by the scruff of my neck, pushed me to the ground with my head under his hand pressed down on the kitchen floor and said 'You do that again, and you will be sorry Finley' He kept my head held down against the floor for a minute or so and then stood up saying to Mom 'That behaviour I will not accept. He needs to learn who is leader of the pack and it's not him! Right I am off.'

And he was gone. I got up, shook myself off, ran outside to our enclosed courtyard and aggressively barking at him as he walked to his car. I know what I did was wrong and it did bring some ill feeling into the house, I just couldn't help myself. Mom later said 'Finley what was that all about? Look, I know you not partial to Ryan, but he is helping us and he was very kind to you this weekend. Please my boy, don't behave like that again. You make things very awkward and difficult for me. If Ryan had treated you badly or unfairly this weekend, I would have been the first to stick up for you. But you make it very difficult to defend you when you bite unsuspecting people on the bum'

She was right. I had misbehaved and he hadn't hurt me when he pushed me to the ground. My pride maybe, but nothing else. I don't know what gets into my head some days. I pick up a scent of something suspicious or someone who could potentially harm my Mom and if they come close to her I lunge at them. I just don't trust men. In all fairness though, Ryan had done nothing. Did I like him? Not particularly, but that was not a reason to bite his bum. I made a another mental note 'Do not bite Ryan's bum again'

Our new days were now filled with meeting Dylan and Maisey for an early morning walk. I liked Maisey very much but she was very aloof and not all that interested in me. Then Mom would come home and job hunt. Late afternoon, I would play with Eddie and Vinnie on the field or we would go through the woodlands before having dinner and settling in for the night.

A few weeks after we had moved in, Mom took me out for a lunchtime walk which was rare. She said she needed to clear her head and couldn't face phoning another company for work. It was demoralizing and she was fed up. From our house to the rugby fields was a short walk. I knew I wouldn't see my friends because it was midday and they mostly came out to play in the evenings.

As we approached the field, Mom saw Debbie who was a dog walker and she had Vinnie with her along with three other dogs I didn't recognise. So I ran at full speed to Debbie. I liked her very much. She thought I was very special and always made a fuss of me and gave me treats she kept in her pocket.

As I approached I saw a tall man with a grey dog who had a white tipped tail and four white socked paws. They were standing talking to Debbie. Oh wow! I liked this man very much. I am not partial to men as you know but, I liked this one. His dog? Not so much at the time, but him? Definitely. I had been introduced to everyone before Mom caught up. Debbie said 'Hello Finley! How are you today? This is Thorn, and his dog called Mrs D. You know Vinnie, and these are Daisy, Rocco and Ragnar'

Mom arrived and said her hello's and Thorn put his hand out to shake Moms and said 'Hello Ma'am, I'm Thorn and this is Mrs D' Mom shook his hand and then the three of them stood back making small talk. Vinnie and his other friends were chasing each other and Vinnie kept calling me to come and play but for the first time, I had no interest in chasing balls. I was taking in all the information I could get on this man, Thorn.

His scent and energy were amazing and he really liked my Mom. I was picking up mixed feelings from mom though. I wasn't sure if she liked him or not. I sidled over to Mrs D 'Hi Mrs D, I'm Finley' and she replied with 'Hello Finley' I heard Thorn telling Mom 'She is a Bearded Collie x Lurcher and sixteen years old. Although she has a few minor lumps and bumps, she is still going strong'

'Wow! That is old!' I said out loud without thinking until I heard Mrs D 'Mind your manners boy!' and muttered under her breath something about the dogs of today having no respect for their elders. She was twelve years older than me. I needed to find out more about this Thorn man so I ignored her comment and pressed on. 'Mrs D, is your Dad single?' I got a niff naff reply like 'Why do you ask?' she was annoyed with me for passing my comment about her age. She felt I had been disrespectful. I was not deterred 'Mrs D, firstly, I am sorry. I never meant to upset you. Secondly I am asking if your Dad is single, because I can see he really likes my Mom and I need to find my Mom a new boyfriend. So, is your Dad single or does he have someone in his life?'

She looked at me with her face all pinched, still annoyed with me over my earlier comment and answered 'Yes he is single. He has a daughter Amber who is twenty-one years old. She lives with us. I am going to move him along now. My Dad can talk for Britain and it's very annoying. I have Doggy News to read and I am done with sniffing the same patch for the past hour. Next time mind your manners and think before you speak.' I apologized again to Mrs D and moved away from her and closer to my Mom. I had really upset her and I didn't mean to.

Mrs D began showing Thorn in no uncertain terms that she had, had enough and wanted to move on. I remember thinking it was lucky for Thorn that he didn't speak dog because Mrs D was really annoyed that he had kept her in the same spot for so long. Mom had also finished with the chatting and wanted to continue our walk. So goodbyes were said and everyone went in a different direction with their dogs.

I couldn't stop thinking of what I had picked up from Thorn. He really did like my Mom. How was I going to make this happen? I would speak to my boys. Mom had her boys, and I now had my own boys, Eddie and Vinnie. I decided to speak to them that evening. Maybe they would have some advice for me. Usually my Mom always talks to herself out loud. So I know what she is thinking, but this time she was silent. So frustrating.

Even after we got home and she spoke to my Nan, and Jessica she mentioned nothing. She tells them everything. Why had she not told my Nan she met Thorn? It was not looking good to me. If he had made an impression on her, surely she would want to talk to my Nan about it? Nothing! Not a single word was mentioned about Thorn.

Faith, was what Barney had told me all those years back. That fat cat's words were ringing in my ears. I decided to create my own vortex to Anubis. I just hoped he wasn't on holiday with God or this was never going to happen.

That same evening my Mom was feeling lazy and didn't feel like taking me out for a walk. I was having none of it. I needed to speak to Eddie and Vinnie to get some ideas. So I pushed and pushed until eventually she said 'Oh dear God Finley! Seriously? You went out this morning for what? An hour? Then again at lunch time for another hour and a half, and you pestering to go out again? You a pain Finley.'

I may be a pain, but she cannot count the lunch time walk, because that was spent watching, listening, and trying to drag information out of Mrs D. Besides, I had my own work to do and I needed to speak to the boys for ideas. This was an important walk.

As I approached the field, I could see no Vinnie and no Eddie. Maybe we had missed them. There were a few dogs I didn't know and I wasn't about to go asking them for advice.

So I had no choice but to wind my neck in and be patient. I didn't know then, but it would be a long time before I saw my friends or Mrs D again.

The days turned into weeks and months. There was so much going on in our lives and our walking times and routine were all out.

Mom had sold her company car to buy an old Mercedes Estate. We used to have one before we left for South Africa. She loved them because of the boot space. That car broke down after a couple of weeks and the cost to repair it was quoted at £5500. Mom was devastated.

She ended up selling it for scrap and got £700. Then she bought another car with Ryan's help, a Citroen Xsara and that broke down after one week and went back to the garage she bought it from for repairs. When she picked it up, it broke down again. She was having a nightmare time with cars that's for sure. It all sorted itself out in the end.

Also Adam, Mom's Dad, was refusing to take his medication for his brain tumor. Esme phoned and said Adam was very aggressive and drinking heavily. Although continuing with his chemo therapy, he was neglecting his health and she was at her wits end.

Then it was all the job hunting and interviews which amounted to nothing. They would all tell her how impressed they were with her knowledge and references. They were very keen to get her on board, and then she would never hear from them again.

In between all of this, we had spotted Thorn walking with Mrs D a few times, but we were too far away and all Mom did was wave and Thorn would wave back. She purposely didn't walk over because she would say 'Finley there is too much going on in my life right now. Seriously it's a mess and I am not in the mood for small chit chat'

I remember the cracks were beginning to show with Mom and Ryan. He was very kind and did help us a lot, but for that, he wanted payment in the form of sex. Mom felt Ryan viewed her as some kind of mistress. He would give her £300 a month to help with her keeping our heads above water, and would buy the odd meal on the weekend he did come, but that was pretty much where it ended.

I would hear her talking to Nan 'Mom, I have not stopped bleeding for months. I need to get around to seeing a doctor. I have period pain nonstop and headaches that are slowly killing me! I sleep with three towels on my bed and Jessica suggested I wear incontinence pads. The last thing I feel like doing is having sex. Ryan is relentless and says when I see him I should want to pleasure him. It's Groundhog day all over again.'

Ryan didn't care how he got 'pleasured' just as long as he was paid for his kindness.

Sometime during all that, and after three hundred failed attempts to find a job that would pay her well, she decided to do Caring. She said to herself 'Perhaps it was time to give something back' She phoned up an agency based not far from us and made arrangements to go for an interview. More or less at the same time, Moms sister Layla said there were a couple of mothers at Willow's school who were desperate for after school care as the waiting list for aftercare at the school was a year long. Layla suggested maybe that was something Mom might be interested in doing.

Mom contacted the two woman who needed help and after they had all met, it was agreed that they would pay her £10 an hour to collect their child from school, give them an early dinner, and personally drop them back at home at 18h00.

Mom asked both the Mothers if the children had any allergies, any health issues she needed to know about, and a list of foods they didn't like. Neither of them had health issues, and by all accounts were easy to feed.

The young boy she would have every day and the little girl was twice a week. Both children were the same age as Willow, 8 years old. That little bit of extra cash in hand money was going to help us enormously and it was really easy for mom because both kids lived on the base. So her, and I, could simply walk them home every evening.

All she had to do now was wait to pass her CRB check which she told me was a criminal check and then she would start the Caring as well.

Mom began picking the children up a couple of weeks before her CRB returned. Although the children finished school at 15h15, Mom and I had to be there by no later than 14h30 or we couldn't find parking. The parents only paid from the time Mom got home which meant they paid for two hours a day. Even though for us it was closer to four hours. So if both children came on the days they were meant to and weren't sick or one of their parents picked them up, then Mom would earn £140 a week. That was a lot of money for us.

I remember her phoning my Nan at the end of the first day with the children and telling her a story about Georgia and Tyler 'Mom I laughed. The kids were a little nervous at first but they very quickly settled in. Tyler was a pleasure. He ate whatever I gave him and wanted to be left alone to play games on his mobile.

Georgia on the other hand, is one very clever little girl and a handful. I set the table for them both. Trying to think of what kids like to eat, and not having any of my own to go by, it's hit and miss. So thinking I am covering all bases, I cooked chicken nuggets, chips, peas and I made a little fresh side salad for each of them followed by a desert and boxed orange juice. I thought I had done a sterling job.

Tyler said thank you and tucked right in cleaning his plate. Georgia says to me, Danny, I don't eat this. My other Nanny who I stay with for three days a week, roasts my chicken. So if you going to give me chicken, please make sure it is roasted because truly, this meal is very unhealthy. I will eat the salad and my dessert, but the rest I am leaving. Also I don't like this juice. It's full of preservatives which are very unhealthy for me. My other

Nanny makes me freshly squeezed juice and can you please put the TV on, I like to watch The Chase!'

My Mom and Nan were in stitches of laughter. Georgia would prove to be one very difficult guest to please. One day she came home with a list she had done in class of all the things she didn't like and was 'allergic' to. Mom passed the list onto Georgia's mother who was mortified and said it was a load of nonsense. Georgia was just testing the boundaries because she had told her Mom, she loved staying with us after school and she had even started playing one Nanny up against the other to get the best out of both her Nannies. Mom just laughed and thanked Georgia's Mother for her feedback.

By now, Mom had started her Caring and was coming home feeling very depressed. It took her ages to settle in and feel comfortable doing the job she was doing. She was very emotional during the first days. Her first call of the day started at 06h30 and her last call was generally at 13h00. Then she would rush home to change out her uniform and race to get to the school in hope of finding a car space.

So I missed all the day time and early evening walks when I may have caught up with Mrs D. Mom would take me out at 05h00 before leaving for work, and again around 19h00 after dropping the kids. Mrs D never went out that early or that late. In fact neither did Vinnie and Eddie. The only people we may bump into is Dylan and Maisey. Otherwise it was now just mom and I. My hope of getting Thorn and Mom together was fading by the day.

Everything stayed like that for ages with not much change, and then Mom had to take a few days off work because her knee was playing up. That same old injury she had back in South Africa had returned. She could walk very slowly but bending, lifting and carrying was out of the question.

It was during that week, when she was taking me out during normal hours again, that we bumped into Eddie, Vinnie and Ragnar. Now was my chance to talk to the boys. After chasing the tennis ball for ages, we finally started settling down and I told the guys the story and asked for their advice. Strangely it was Ragnar who gave me the best advice. Ragnar was a rescue from Romania and very wise for his young years.

'Finley, it's easy. Why don't you speak to Mrs D and ask her to let you know every time her, and Thorn are going out for a walk. Your Mom doesn't understand dog, so she won't understand what the barking is all about. After Mrs D has given you the signal, then you start pestering her until she gives in and out you both go and by pure chance you bump into Thorn. Easy peasy'

'Ragnar, you are one super smart dog. That is the best plan ever! Thank you. Now all I have to do is wait to see Mrs D again and I can put my plan into action.' I told him. I was over the moon. So we did more running around before our parents called time out and we all made our way home. I was also still waiting to race against Gordie, but because of Moms work hours my Nan had not been around to visit. Instead Mom would stop in at Nan during her day time calls.

That night after Ragnar's advice, Mom was on the phone to my Nan 'My knee is playing up. Dammit man. I went through this in South Africa. It's swollen and terribly painful. It's all the bending I do during the day. Caring is back breaking work. I have gained all the respect in the world for the people who do this job day in and year out for so little money. They truly are undervalued and it's utterly shameful. For me it is rewarding and sad in equal measures. I have one old man that I have to get out of bed every day, undress him, give him a wash, put a clean nappy on, dress him and get him comfortable until the lunch time Carer arrives. This old man was a pilot in the Second World War. What must this proud man think and feel having me wash his private parts and clean his bum? He has most of his faculties but the body is breaking down. My heart breaks for these old people.'

She went on to tell Nan 'I also have a young woman who is my first call of the day at 06h30. She is only twenty six and she is crippled from Cerebral Palsy. She baths herself believe it or not, but I have to dress her, put a sanitary towel in her panties if it's that time of the month and put splints on her legs. This young girl is the most positive woman I have ever met. She puts me to shame. I am embarrassed to complain about a damn thing in my life after working with these incredible individuals who have such strength and resilience. It is truly a humbling experience'

Then the inevitable question from my Nan 'how are things with Ryan?' the answer on that day was 'Mom, it's not going well. We not fighting or arguing but I feel coming here for Ryan is a chore. He feels obliged to come over and is gone at first light on a Sunday. There is zero communication between us and although thankfully he now is no longer interested in being intimate with me, he does want to be pleasured as payment for coming over and the help he gives me. It is a very unhealthy set up on all levels.

We are worlds apart. He never asks how I am, how my job is going, nothing. We sit for the whole time he is here in silence or I am the one trying to form a conversation and I get one syllable answers. It's quite frankly a waste of life for both of us. I really need to talk to him'

Nothing my Mom said that night to Nan came as a surprise. I was just glad she was beginning to see the light. Ryan's visits had gone from a weekly Friday to Sunday, to Saturday afternoon leaving on Sunday morning, to every other weekend. It was clear even to me that this was going backwards.

Mom had asked Ryan several times, 'Ryan where is this going? Do you see us actually rebuilding a home together?' and Ryan would always answer with 'Stop putting pressure on me! I am happy with the way thing are. We don't need to live in each other's pockets and I can't say if I will ever consider building a home with you the way things are. You have reverted back to your old ways of withholding sex from me and that worries me.'

Ryan had a way of twisting and turning everything Mom said. It was his gift she would say. So I wasn't surprised to finally hear her saying that she needed to talk to him. It was a conversation overdue. I could sense that it wouldn't be much longer and all this would be done and dusted.

After her week of sick leave, it was back to work for Mom. It didn't last long. She probably got through a week and was home again and this time for good. After seeing the doctor, he told her she would have to quit doing Caring because she was heading for a knee replacement if she didn't. So she phoned her work and reluctantly resigned.

So in Moms words 'it is back to the drawing board' one good thing though was she still had the kids after school and that was bringing in that weekly money that kept us afloat. I know it wasn't easy on my Mom but it was so nice to have her home during the day again. We were back to our normal walking routine. If I ever did see Mrs D, it was still always at a distance. There was nothing I could do. I had to just wait for my opportunity.

Just before Christmas, two things happened. Ryan put a dog flap for me in the lounge door leading to the garden, which was amazing. I was a little nervous of it at first, but once I realized I could fly in and out at top speed barking outside, and then inside, I was very happy. Also it stopped the moaning from Mom about having to keep the door open and paying the gas bill to heat the garden!

The second thing was I finally got to race against Gordie. That day I remember like it was yesterday. There was a score to settle and loads of treats up for grabs. Mom and Nan took us down to the rugby pitch for a walk. My Nan struggles to walk, so she usually sits on the bench and Mom takes Gordon and I onto the field and throws the ball for us both.

We were both on the far side of the pitch. It was a straight run for us from one side of the pitch to where my Nan was sitting. Gordie and I squared up. Gordon was reminding me 'When I win Finley, remember, I get your tripe sticks and your marrow bone!' and I was saying 'Gordie my friend, when you lose, I get your pigs ear and that menthol dental stick if you haven't eaten it already!'

Gordon said he had eaten that dental stick but he had recently stashed a new one under my Nans bed which I could have. I loved those menthol sticks. My Mom didn't buy those. The pigs ear I wasn't all that fond of, but I knew they were Gordon's favourite, so that is why I included the ear into our bet.

We both looked at the hundred meter plus run that lay ahead of us to my Nans bench. We did our own count down and we were off. For the first twenty-five meters or so, Gordie was ahead of me. For his size he was damn fast and I must be honest, I had my doubts on whether I had made a mistake challenging him. My Mom and Nan were watching us and had no idea what we were running at full pelt for. Neither of us wanted to lose this race.

We hit the half way mark and it was around that distance that I peeked and managed to maintain control of my speed. Gordon on the other hand was slowing down. He had run a good race and make no mistake, he was fast. But he lacked the endurance and wasn't built to do the long distances that I am. That was my advantage. Once in this zone, I can run for miles.

Poor Gordon was devastated. When we started this bet, I really didn't have a clue who would win. We both teased each other and put our treats up for grabs but neither of us really had an idea of who would be quicker on the day.

When we got home after the race, I said to Gordon 'Gords, here is your tripe stick'

'But I didn't win' replied Gordon

'I know, but you still damn fast. At one point I thought you had me beaten. You quick Gordon. It was fun. Eat your tripe stick, but remember you owe me a menthol dental stick next time I come to you and Nan' I told him

'Geez Fin thanks. You were really fast. You still a Heffalump with three and a half legs but you damn fast! Well done for winning Finley and thanks for the tripe stick mate' barked Gords who loved to tease me about my three and a half legs. I have walked with a limp since I broke my leg, but Gordon agreed, it had certainly not affected my performance. I was the king of speed and well chuffed even though my leg was now really sore.

After Nan and Gordon had gone, life was back to normal. Christmas arrived quickly and Mom always bought me tasty goodies which she wrapped and put under the tree. I could smell the treats and it used to drive me crazy not being able to rip into the paper like I did the mail every day.

Ryan came over for Christmas day. He cooked Mom a lovely roast lamb with veg and I was given the bone which was like heaven. Ryan only stayed for Christmas day and evening. Following day he left to go back home telling Mom he had chores to do. In fact we never saw him again until middle, to late January of the New Year because he had taken three weeks leave and wanted to spend it at home 'doing chores and relaxing. I am entitled to that at least am I not?' he asked Mom.

It was after Ryan had left and just before New Year that Mom bumped into Thorn and Mrs D while out walking. I was over the moon to see Mrs D. I had loads of questions to ask her and I wanted to discuss my future plan that I had been carrying around in my head for way too long now. The one Ragnar had given me. So while Mom and Thorn were talking and agreeing it had been ages since they last saw each other, Mrs D and I got to talking.

She told me Thorn still had no one in his life. That he spoke about my Mom on an almost daily basis and had turned down all offers of meeting someone else. According to Mrs D, her Dad was lonely and very depressed. Mrs D said every time without fail when they went out he would look for mom. They sometimes saw us from a distance and that would cheer him up.

Being mindful of my manners and knowing how important manners were to Mrs D, I very carefully and gently told her of my talk with Ragnar and what he had suggested. Much to my surprise, she agreed it was a good idea and agreed to work with me. The concern I shared was, would I hear her barking? She told me if I looked diagonally from our garden gate, I would see their house. I didn't know what diagonally meant but I gathered it was close. Mrs D said it would take my Mom one minute to walk there. They had seen us going home one day and her Dad had said 'So that's where Danny and Finley live'

Our plan was set. Mrs D would bark letting me know when she was going for a walk and I would do the same for her. That way we would get our parents out and onto the field where they would accidently bump into each other. Plans all made, I left Mrs D to her Doggy News and I ran back to my Mom to hear what her, and Thorn were talking about.

Mom was telling Thorn where she was born, how long she had been in the UK and Thorn was telling Mom he was divorced, ex Armed Forces, retired now from being injured on duty, and living at number fourteen. Mom told him we live at number sixty-nine but she didn't know that he already had that information. Mrs D had just told me.

They seemed to be enjoying their chat and lots of laughing was exchanged which brought Mrs D wobbling back over 'Gosh! I haven't heard my Dad laugh for ages. I admit to liking your Mom, Finley. She has a kind smell. I can see why my Dad is taken with her.' I thanked her and told her I hadn't seen my Mom so relaxed for a very long time either.

As usual though, Mrs D was now restless and wanted to move so she could read the News under the far trees. Thorn reluctantly gave in to Mrs D's demands and said to Mom 'Ma'am it was lovely to see you and talk to you again. Would you like to bump into Mrs D and myself for a walk tomorrow at say lunch time?'

Say yes, say yes! I was barking at my Mother. Mom started laughing and said to Thorn 'He is too clever for his own good! Yes Thorn that sounds lovely. I will see you both on the field around 1pm'

And with that we said our goodbyes. I barked after Mrs D 'Bye Mrs D. Thank you Mrs D. See you tomorrow Mrs D' she looked up from her paper, smiled, put her head down and carried on reading. Mom and I went on a longer walk after that and when we got home she phoned my Nan.

'Hi Mom. I have met such a nice bloke. His name is Thorn and he has an old dog called Mrs D. He also lives on the base' My Nan answered with 'Oh Danny be careful. The last time I visited you, I noticed some unsavory looking people. You don't want to get involved with the wrong man. Be careful my girl.'

I was so frustrated. It was times like this, I wished I could speak human. My Nan had the wrong idea entirely and I was so upset that she may change my Moms mind.

Mom just told Nan 'No Mom he is not like that. He is Armed Forces, my age, and a really decent bloke. There is something strangely familiar about him. I have met him a few times while out walking but it's not that. I feel like I know him, maybe from another life, I know it's crazy. Anyway, look, nothing will come of it. I still need to sort things out with Ryan, but he is never here for me to talk to!'

To which my Nan replied 'Does Ryan not come around anymore?' and Mom told her he was on three weeks leave but he didn't want to come over because he wanted to enjoy his time off doing his chores. My Nan said 'You really are a very silly girl Danny. That is all I am saying on the matter'

Next day as arranged we met up with Thorn and Mrs D. Thorn asked her if he could take her for a little lunch, or a cup of tea and my Mother declined saying 'Thorn that is very kind of you and thank you, but I am in a relationship and have been on and off now for fourteen years.' Thorn went on to ask Mom what she meant by on and off. Mom was honest and told Thorn 'We have had an extremely tumultuous relationship.

This time around it will be a year next month that we have been seeing each other every other weekend. Thorn it's a mess and a long story. As much as I appreciate the invite, at this point in time, I cannot say yes. I hope you understand.'

'Yes Ma'am I think I do. I was married to the female version of your Ryan for twenty years! Ma'am there is so much I could tell you and talk to you about, but perhaps now as you say, is not the right time. All I will say Ma'am, is it took me twenty years to walk away from that. It would be a shame to see you give away another six years before you find the courage to be true to yourself.'

I couldn't believe there were lady Ryan's. I thought it was a man thing and here was Thorn who also had a Ryan in his life. They had both gone quiet. Just standing looking at each other in silence. Mom broke it by saying 'Thorn, thank you for understanding. I need to go now because I need to prepare for the children I look after in the afternoons.'

Thorn replied with 'Ma'am it is my pleasure. Please stay strong. My phone is at home on charge, but take down my number and if you ever need me please just call. May I give you a hug?' After giving my Mom a big hug and her taking Thorns mobile number she said it was the best hug she had ever had. Mrs D and I said our goodbyes and she promised to let me know when they were next heading out.

Mrs D was true to her word. Every time her, and Thorn were on their way out, she would duly let me know. I in turn would pester Mom and out we would go. Our plan worked out too well! Mom was bumping into Thorn on a daily basis and couldn't understand why. Although they would walk and talk and appeared to be enjoying each other's company, my Mom grew suspicious.

We had moved into our new house in the May and it was now January of the New Year and in all that time she had bumped into Thorn a dozen times if that. Now she had seen him a dozen times in two weeks! One evening after we got back she poured a glass of wine and said to me 'Something is not right Finley. I think Thorn is stalking me. Seriously! How is it possible that every single time I leave the front door, I bump into that man? It makes no sense to me. I am beginning to feel like he is watching my every move and its making me feel damn uncomfortable.'

She told the same story to my Nan and Jessica. On one of the following days and using some of the money she had earned from the children, she came home with outdoor security cameras for the front and the back of the house. Which proved that poor Thorn was not stalking her.

Mom was rattled all the same and I was now being instructed to hide behind trees with her. Mrs D would let me know they were out and what direction they were walking, and if Mom saw Thorn or caught site of Mrs D's white tipped tail, she would hide behind a tree, call me and drag me in the opposite direction.

I personally don't think listening to her talking to herself at home, that she knew how to deal with her feelings for Thorn. She was loyal to the 'Ryan cause' and she still hadn't seen him or had the opportunity to talk to him, and as such, she felt that by meeting and talking to Thorn, she was committing the cardinal sin.

Following days when Mrs D would call me and give me directions on where they were heading, I would bark back telling her it was a no go from my side. My Mom was being scared off and I would have to let a few walks go by to calm her nerves down.

It was around Mid Jan when she got an invite to an interview for a company based in London. Mom was very excited and it was a very well paid position back in her industry. The only snag was she would have to take two trains and three tubes to get to work every day and the same on the way home. Which meant she had to be on the station at 06h30 and would only be home around the 19h00 mark in the evening.

She was telling my Nan 'Mom it's not going to be easy. I am going to ask Dylan if he will pick Finley up and walk him with Maisey twice a day. He has his dog flap so he can use that if need be but if I get offered this job I have to take it. I am in no position to be fussy. I am in debt to Ryan and I am desperate for financial independence. I can't carry on like this.'

My Nan asked her what she was going to do with the children and Mom said she would just be honest with the parents and hopefully they would understand her situation. Besides, over the past few weeks Tyler was now being picking up from school by his Dad and Georgia's Mom had started picking her up from school and working from home. So Mom's money had gone from £140 a week to some weeks £60 and others £20. We were struggling financially and the parents were trying to save money where they could. Everyone seemed to be counting their pennies and trying to cut unnecessary spending.

Mom got offered the job which she was over the moon about and Dylan agreed to look after me during the day. So Mom cut him a key for our house and spent some money on a few new shirts for work and a pair of comfortable shoes that she could walk in and that looked good at the same time.

The evening she spoke to Ryan she spoke to the parents. Both sets of parents understood and congratulated Mom. So it all worked out rather well. No hard feelings at all. They thanked Mom for taking such good care of their children which made Mom feel good.

Ryan was very happy. He said he was pleased because he didn't know how much longer he could continue to pay her £300 a month and that he didn't have unlimited resources.

It was all falling into place except my plan with Thorn. The only way I could tell Mrs D what was going on, was by barking the story over from the back yard. My mom would come out and tell me to be quiet, and I would stop mid conversation. Give it a few minutes and start again before being told to stop my nonsense. It took me a whole day to bark the story over to Mrs D. I got into a lot of trouble that day for being so disobedient. Had Mom just left me alone to bark, it would have been over in five minutes.

Now I had no choice but to just hope that Anubis had got all my vortex messages. Our future was now out of my hands and in Moms God and Anubis's hands. I was certainly no longer in control. I would have to use that old thing called 'Faith' that Barney had told me about.

It was now the end of January and a month since Ryan had been over for a weekend. Mom was starting work on the first working day of February and Ryan cancelled his weekend, saying he was working and had to be at the airport to collect his boss and it wasn't worth coming over for the evening because he wouldn't be able to have a drink and relax. He told mom he would be around the following weekend.

Mom started her new job and Dylan was around every morning to pick me up. He would take Maisey and I for long walks through the woods. I also played a lot with Vinnie and Eddie. It was bitterly cold and we were experiencing a heavy snow fall which I loved. Dylan felt awful leaving me at home by myself, so he would take me home with him and Maisey. After giving us a breakfast, we would all lie on the sofa and watch TV until the lunch time walk.

Then around 18h30 every evening, Dylan would walk me home knowing it was only a few minutes and Mom would be home to feed me dinner. He was really good to me and Mom was very grateful to Dylan. Most evenings, even though Mom new Dylan had walked me, we would go out for a short walk. Mom said it cleared her head from her day and besides, snow was our thing. Every year when it snowed we had the best fun ever. She would make snow balls for me to catch and she would throw them at me. I would chase her, barking before she pelted me with another snow ball.

I did see Mrs D on a few occasions while out and about. We did manage to have our talk about Mom and Thorn, but she agreed that our paws were tied to our tail.

She told me Thorn is taking terrible strain and that he had seen Mom hiding behind the trees and bushes and couldn't understand why. Dylan told Thorn that Mom had started a new job in London and he was looking after me during the day. I could see that Thorn was really low but there was truly nothing more I could do. After the first week of Mom starting work, Ryan came over. I could sense being with us was the last thing he felt like doing but he was with us all the same. He and Mom spoke about her job and how she was going to sort her finances out and look at paying him back.

That weekend, was to be our last with Ryan. I was curled up asleep on my bed in the lounge and Ryan walked past me and was pushing me with his feet. I'd open my eyes and he would stop. Then I would close my eyes and he would begin nudging me again and pushing me with his feet. Mom saw this and asked him 'What are you doing? Why are you doing that to Finley? He is sleeping' and Ryan answered with 'He needs to know what it feels like to be bugged when you trying to relax. When we watching TV he comes over for attention and its annoying. He needs to learn what it feels like to have someone bugging you all the time'

My Mom was very irritated with Ryan and told him to stop doing that and grow up. Ryan told Mom she had no sense of humour and besides she spoilt me too much. At the end of the day I was a dog and nothing more. That evening, Mom let it all go, but the following morning after Ryan had surfaced and they had drunk a cup of tea she said to Ryan 'We need to talk'

'Jesus you not going to go down the same road again of expecting everything overnight from me are you? I am really not in the mood for this shit.' replied Ryan.

Mom just sat there quietly for a while and then answered 'No. We not going down the same old road again. I have met someone else. Nothing has happened, but there is the hope, the dream, of a happy relationship and future. I always said to you that if the day ever came when I met someone, I would let you know. That day is now. I cannot carry on like this anymore. You and I are not in love with each other. It's become a habit. If I am wrong, now is the time to talk to me'

Much to both our surprise, Ryan actually agreed and said 'Thank you for your honesty Danny and yes, I am not in love with you either. That doesn't mean I don't still want sex with you, but you want hearts and flowers and I cannot give that. What I can offer is not enough for you. Shame really, I enjoyed our sex. Oh well, we need to sort out the money repayments from the past year I have been supporting you but that can be done another time. I have to get my shopping done and I have things to do at home. So I will leave you in peace'

Ryan was packed in minutes and final goodbyes were exchanged. From start to finish it must have been ten minutes at the most. Unbelievable for me, but it was finally over. Mom then phoned Nan 'It's over and I feel like a weight has been lifted from my shoulders. I never realized what an emotional burden I was carrying nor how heavy it was. Ryan was for once, honest. I am going to get on with my life now. At least we didn't end screaming and insulting each other like we have done every other time'

My Nan told Mom she had done the right thing and Mom just said to my Nan 'Mom it was a long overdue conversation' While she was talking to Nan, a message came through so she read it while talking to my Nan and said 'God almighty, you can't make this up. The man is something else. He has just sent me a message asking me if I want sex with him. Do I want him to turn around and come back for no strings attached sex'

That wouldn't be the last of the messages. I remember a few weeks later he sent Mom a message asking her if she would be interested in an affair. Mom told him she was dating Thorn and all he said was, he would make it worth her while, it would be their secret liaison. My Mom muttered something about him needing to fuck off and leave her alone.

The same morning Ryan left, Mom took me out for a walk and we almost bumped into Thorn and Mrs D, but Mom yanked my collar pulling me behind the tree and telling me to 'Shush' We waited there until they had turned the corner and Mom began pulling me in the opposite direction.

Her behaviour was really strange. I had no idea when or how this was going to change. The new week began, and it was back to Dylan, Maisey and myself during the day, and Mom and I in the evening.

By pure chance we did bump into Thorn one evening during that second week. I had not let Mrs D know and it really was by chance they were out walking. Thorn congratulated Mom on her new job and when Mom questioned how he knew, he said Dylan had mentioned it. He asked Mom how she was and she told him she was doing well. When Thorn asked her about Ryan, she told him they had broken up a few days ago. Thorn asked Mom if she would like to go over to his house for a tea.

No was the answer and she just said 'Thanks Thorn, but no. I really just need time out and to be on my own. Maybe next time' After we got home from that walk Jessica phoned to check up on Mom and once Mom had finished telling Jessica the whole story Jessica said to Mom 'Danny, you should have shown Ryan the door and taken your key back a long time ago. You tried, it didn't work out, end of! It's now time to move on. You are so much stronger this time around and I can hear there is no pain or hurt in your voice which is a great start to a new life. I would bet my bottom dollar that Ryan has another woman or several in his life. Good riddance I say! What I don't understand is why you turned down the offer of tea with Thorn.'

Mom replied with 'I am not upset in the least regarding Ryan. I have wanted to do this for ages, but felt obliged to keep trying. I can't explain it. Doesn't make any sense to me either. I think it was the familiarity. Who knows? It certainly wasn't his £300 because I have not been drawing on that for a few months now. It's all still in his bank account. Before I got this new job I was working a few hours every weekend at the local shop down the road and they pay me cash in hand. Look it's not much, but it has helped me to not draw on Ryan's money.'

'I am impressed. I hadn't realized you were doing that. However, it still doesn't explain why you turning Thorn down. Tell me you not still hiding behind trees!' Jessica interjected.

Mom was laughing and said 'Yes, I am still hiding behind trees! Jessica, the truth is I am scared. I have not had anyone new in my life for many, many years. I am terrified of getting up close and personal. I have health issues as you know. How the hell do I start a new relationship not being in a position to get intimate? Urgh the whole idea of getting naked and sharing my body with someone new is driving me crazy. Besides, what if he turns out to be another 50 Shades of Grey? For that reason, and because I really do like him, I am still hiding'

It was Jessica's turn to laugh 'Danny no one says you have to jump straight into bed with the man. I know it's how dating is done these days, but that has never been you.

Just take things slowly, date. In that time you can explain your health issues and if he cannot accept that, then he is not the man for you. He is another cock struck prick whose only interest is putting another notch on his bed post. However, if he is half the man, I think he may be, he will understand and support you until you are in a position to be more physical. Not all men are assholes. Believe it or not, there are some good ones out there. It's a cup of tea for God sake. At least go and see what he is all about! How is your new job going?'

'You right, I should probably just go over for a cup of tea and stop hiding behind trees and bushes. But if he tries anything, or suggests anything sexual, that will be the last he ever sees or hears from me. My job is OK. It's a very young company I work for and I feel like a fossil. They all very bright and brilliant at their job. I like them. Problem is they all like to go out after work for drinks and I keep turning then down. Jessica I just can't do it. I finish work at 5 o' clock and it takes me almost two hours to get home. I have Finley who has been waiting all day with Dylan. I have responsibilities that these other guys who all live local to the office don't have. Other than that? I am enjoying it.' Mom told Jessica

'Well they need to understand that. Which I am sure they do. Have you explained the reasons why you keep turning them down for drinks?' Jessica asked

'Of course I have. Look its only week two, so let's see how things pan out. I am hoping that once my probation is over, I can work more from home. This travelling into London every day is dreadful.' Replied Mom

'As you say, get through the probation and things will change. The daily trip you make to the office and back is awful. I have been there and done that too. Danny, it's time to go for that cup of tea and to begin a new chapter of your life story.' And on that note Jessica said her goodbyes and they agreed to catch up in a few days' time.

Mom didn't go for the cup of tea. Instead we went around to Dylan for dinner which was very nice. Mom didn't feel threatened by Dylan and there was no interest on either side other than friendship. Mom took over a thank you card and a gift for Dylan. They chatted about life and Dylan laughed at Moms stories about hiding from Thorn.

He told Mom 'you one crazy bloody woman. He is such a decent bloke. I see him all the time and we have had long talks and he is as genuine as they come. If I were a woman I would be beating the man's door down!'

They laughed, ate and Mom made Dylan promise that he would not betray her trust by telling Thorn that she hides behind trees. Dylan laughed his head off and told her he was insulted that she would even think he would do something like that. Mom had a couple of glasses of wine and then we said our goodbye and walked home. Mom had work the next day and didn't want to wake up with a headache.

The rest of that week went without any glitches. On the Saturday, Mom sent Thorn a message 'Hi Thorn, if your offer of a cuppa still stands, I would love to accept xx' the reply came through almost immediately 'The kettle is on Ma'am xx'

I was over the moon. Finally things were moving in the right direction. Anubis must have got my vortex messages. Mom got dressed, gave me a brushing and we both went out looking for number fourteen and were shocked to find it so close to our house. You would think numbers fourteen and sixty-nine would be far apart, but in fact Mrs D was right. From our back yard, you could see Thorns house.

Mom was very tense. I could see it in her energy and she was walking very slowly. Thorn greeted us at the garden gate. Gave Mom a hug, greeted me warmly, kissed my face, and served Mom tea at the outside table and chairs. When Mom sat down, I went on search for Mrs D. I found her asleep on her bed by the front door. She told me she was not feeling very well and would rather be left alone today. Minding my manners as Mrs D had always reminded me to do, I apologized for disturbing her and went back to Mom and Thorn.

I did notice that the house was a mess. My Mom was such a fussy woman. Everything had its place and if I didn't move I would have been vacuumed up years ago and tossed in the bin. There was seldom a dirty teaspoon in our house. All I can say, is thank Anubis my Mother never needed the toilet while having her tea. She would have fainted had she seen what I did.

I was worried about Mrs D. Although I knew her to be very grumpy and very straight talking, she really didn't look very well to me and it made me sad.

It was while we were sitting at Thorn that Mom's Dad, Adam, phoned her. After the call Mom apologized to Thorn and explained that her Dad had brain cancer. He had already had one op that he was lucky to come out alive from. Now he had decided to go in for another op on his tumour in the hope that the surgeon would give him a little longer to live.

Thorn told Mom his father had died of a cancerous brain tumour as well and that his father had withered away to nothing and within two months of the operation, was dead. I didn't like Adam as you know, but I couldn't help but feel sad for the suffering he was going through. I also heard Mom mention many times that perhaps it was the tumour that had changed him and turned him into an unbearable man. I guess we will never know for sure.

That first day, Mom didn't want to over stay her welcome. So I think it was after her second or third cup of tea, she said to Thorn 'Thank you for the tea, the company and the chat. I have really enjoyed my little visit but I have shopping to do and a house to clean. So Fin and I will leave you in peace to enjoy the rest of your Saturday'

Thorn didn't want Mom to go but he reluctantly gave her a hug and told her to have a good day too and if she felt like some company, to just come over. She didn't need to phone, or message, the door he would leave open for her. He knelt down, gave me a hug, and kiss followed up with 'Finley look after your mom for me please' I licked his face, wagged my tail, and he knew, I would do exactly that.

I liked Thorn so much. I trusted him with my life and I can't begin to tell you how happy I was that he was finally being acknowledged by Mom. She had broken the ice and I hoped we wouldn't be hiding behind any more trees and bushes.

That day I remember there was nothing to clean up. There never was in Moms house. She washed and packed away as she cooked, swept the floor ten times a day and vacuumed at least twice a day to keep my hair off everything. She used to say 'Jesus Finley, when I crack open an egg I find your hair inside!'

All we did that day was go for a long walk and stopped in at my Nan for a quick visit. I got to have a chat with Gordon and tell him all about Thorn and we were off again before Gordon had chance to tell me about the latest historical documentary he had watched.

The following day we were out at our normal times. We didn't see Thorn or Mrs D on our first walk but I could sense the change in my Mom. I instinctively knew the hiding behind bushes was over. She was walking freely and in fact, I noticed her scouring the fields for any sign of Thorn. She was disappointed to not have bumped into him. I smiled to myself.

Later that Sunday mom received a message from Thorn. He was going to have a BBQ with his daughter Amber and invited us to join them. She actually said yes! That was a lovely afternoon. Her, and Thorn chatted for hours on end. They were laughing and singing along to music being played. I heard Mom asking Thorn if she could use the toilet. I had noticed the house was a lot tidier than it had been the day before.

While she was gone, I got talking to Mrs D who told me it wasn't Thorn who was untidy it was Amber. She told me Thorn pulls his hair out cleaning after Amber. It's a never ending cycle of mess. So Amber was the grub! Well, grubby or not, I liked her.

As the evening came, Thorn asked Mom for a dance and they danced on the lawn to 'I've got you under my skin' by Frank Sinatra. In all my growing up years and being with Ryan, I had never once seen my Mom dance with him. I had never heard Ryan laugh, let alone sing. This was an incredible experience for me. This was a side I had never seen of my Mom.

Yes her, and I often listened to music and she would hold my front legs and we would dance, but I had never seen her laugh and dance with another human being. All I ever saw her doing with Ryan was either fighting, crying, or both.

Even Mrs D said 'Well that is a first. I have been with my Dad for 16 years and never seen him dance barefoot on the lawn and so happy with anyone before. He never did this with my last Mother. All they did was fight, argue and then he would be sent out the Country again for another few months'

It was a first for both Mrs D and myself and one that had made an impression on us.

That following week was another bad one for Mom. She went to work on the Monday after dancing with Thorn the night before and was called into a meeting. This was the third week of working. Her boss said 'Danny, we all like you very much, and your work is excellent, but all of us feel you just not fitting in. We have invited you out so many times, and we just feel you don't want to be part of the team. We are a company that believe in socializing to maintain working relations and it's not working out for us. So I am sorry. As a gesture of good will, I will pay you a full salary for the next three months, but after our meeting, feel free to pack up and leave when you ready.'

Mom did try and explain that she lived a two hour trip away and that she had me waiting at home and she simply wasn't in a position to stay out late after work. She had too many commitments. Her boss said he understood, but it didn't change the fact that they didn't feel she was the right fit for their organization.

Chapter 11

Mom was really shocked at losing her job and scratched her head many times over the reasons that were given to her. She simply couldn't get her head around it. In fact no one she spoke to could. She would ask the question often 'How can a person be fired for not socialising enough?'

Whatever their reasons were for getting rid of Mom, she was beyond grateful for the next three months' salary. It was a breather for her and it would give her three months to find another job and three months before having to sign onto Universal Credits.

Thorn was coming over almost every day which was fantastic. In fact our life seemed to be on fast forward. Mom and Thorn just fit like a paw in a hand. It's a dog thing. When we meet someone new, and they ask us for our paw, it's a strange thing, sometimes, you give your paw to a human and the fit is uncomfortable. Their hand is too small. It's too big. Or just doesn't feel right. Sometimes even with the right fit, the energy that you pick up from that persons hand is unpleasant, so you pull your paw away.

Well my Mom and Thorn were the right paw and hand size and they had a wonderful energy together. They just seemed to light up a room when they walked in. They were so happy. It was one of those early evenings while out on a walk when Thorn asked Mom why she hid behind trees and bushes.

Mom gasped 'Oh my God! You saw me?'

'Of course I saw you! It is Krav Maga self-defence. 'Perception of environment' and one of the most important mental skills you develop is situational awareness.' Thorn was laughing at mom's reaction.

'Krav Maga? Situational Awareness? Sometimes you had your back to me so how would you have known or seen me? Did Dylan tell you? Oh God I am so embarrassed!'

'No Ma'am, Dylan never said a word. Krav Maga is a worldwide self-defence training which empowers people with skills to be safer and stronger. Part of that training is Situational Awareness. You trained to use the face of your phone, your watch, your glasses, looking at the eyes of approaching people, take note of your feelings and listen. It's a lot to try and explain. For example, if you can, always position yourself where you have your back protected so you can best see approaching threats. A hundred and fifty years ago and more, it was called the 'Gunfighters Seat' Thorn was laughing

That evening Thorn pointed out every tree and bush we had hidden behind. My Mom was horrified and covered her eyes with her hands. She kept apologizing and Thorn would just laugh and tell her not to be silly. Her hiding he had found amusing. The only thing he needed to understand was why.

Mom explained why. Telling him she felt guilty about Ryan and didn't want to do anything that would cause pain, blame or shame. She had to end things with Ryan first. Then she told him she thought that he was stalking her because they kept bumping into each other and it seemed every time she left her house there he was! Also she was terrified of getting intimate and she told him about her health issues.

Thorn was very calm and told Mom 'Ma'am if it wasn't so serious, I would burst out laughing. But for you to hide behind trees and hedges, it was very real for you. So, number one, I understand entirely about Ryan. You behaved honourably. Number two, I was never stalking you. I too was amazed that every time I left my house it would be minutes later and you rounded the corner. I wonder if Finley and Mrs D don't have anything to do with this. Yes you, two! Don't stand there with that innocent look. You both capable of pulling something like this off!' said Thorn while bending down and ruffling our coats.

I was wagging my body and Mrs D was quietly laughing. If only they knew!

Mom was laughing while he continued 'Number three, I am not with you to notch up another mark on my bed post. I am here for the long haul. I would never, ever, force myself on you, nor put you in a position whereby you felt uncomfortable. Of course I enjoy being intimate, but I am by no means ruled by that. It is not at the top of my priority list. I don't need to be intimate with you to be happy. You will get no pressure from me sexually and that is my word of honour'

'Thank you Thorn' is all mom said

'Ma'am there is nothing to thank me for. I will be with you every step of the way. That is if you want me to. While you sort your medical issues out. Please, never feel obliged or under pressure to do anything you are not ready or comfortable to do. No man on this earth has the right to demand or expect, anything from any woman. I find men who demand sex, or abuse their wives or partners, either emotionally or physically, abhorrent!'

Most of the time Thorn would come over to our house. Mom just felt more comfortable in our space. During this time she also discovered it was not only Amber who was grubby. Which Mrs D and I laughed about many times. Then again, Mrs D while laughing asked me one day 'Is my Dad grubby? Or is your Mom over the top tidy?' Good point really and one I didn't have the answer to.

When Thorn came over, they would sit in the garden. He would light a fire, they would have music playing in the back ground and they would just talk. Mrs D and I, got to share many stories about our life. She loved Thorn very much and as such, a little jealousy crept into the old girl.

Every time I went near Thorn, Mrs D would arise from the dead, wobble over on her noodle legs and nip me. I used to just laugh because she never hurt me. I would say to her 'Oi! What was that for? I did nothing!'

'I helped you get our parents together, I did not do this for you to take my Dad. You get enough love and affection from your Mom.'

'Oh common Mrs D. I could never take your place. You have been with your Dad for sixteen years. His loyalty will always lie with you. I love him too and all I want is just a little bit of his attention and affection. No one is taking anything or anyone away. You really do need to calm down' I would tell her.

It took Mrs D a long time to truly accept me and realise that my intentions were innocent. To be fair, we had both grown up as a single dog and when I saw my Mother giving Mrs D kisses and brushing her coat, or giving her treats, I also got a twinge. I too could be jealous and just push my way in front of Mrs D losing my manners and gaining a nip along the way.

In the early days, Mrs D and I had our issues, but we soon sorted all that out and she came to realise that I was no threat and that we could share the love for our parents.

Mom asked Thorn at least a hundred times to please call her Danny and Thorn would reply with 'Yes Ma'am' He simply couldn't do it. In the end she gave up asking him because he simply found it too uncomfortable. So he agreed to drop the Ma'am and my Mom has now become 'Sir' When she moans at Thorn about anything he always replies with 'Yes Sir, Ma'am, Sir' and they burst out laughing.

We did so much when Thorn came into our lives. I went on my first fishing camping trip. Thorn is a big Carp Fisherman and with Mom loving outdoors, she was the perfect guest for his fishing weekend. It was the most exciting thing for me. We arrived at this stunning secluded lake. Thorn put the tent up, sorted the inside of the tent out. Then he put up an awning for outside with two chairs, a table, sorted the BBQ out put a tin kettle on the fire to make a cup of tea for Mom.

Next up was his fishing rods. These are fancy things that beep and make all sorts of sounds. I love them. Every time the alarm would go off I would run past the rods and into the water to see what the fuss was all about. Invariably getting tangled up in the fishing line. Thorn would then have to unwrap me from his line. I came to realise rather quickly, this was not what I was meant to do.

Thorn never raised his voice once at me. It was my Mom who did the shouting and telling me off for disturbing the lines and chasing the fish away. Thorn just laughed 'Sir, don't be so hard on him. It's exciting for him. He doesn't understand that he is destroying any hope of me catching a fish. He will learn in time. It's his first camping trip. Go easy on the boy'

'You clearly have no idea how much Finley likes fishing!' then Mom told him the stories about my fishing in the boys ponds back in South Africa and how bloody minded I can be. I was not impressed she had told Thorn about my bad behaviour. So I made the decision to show him, she was wrong. I did have will power. I would simply do my own fishing, in the space next to Thorn and then no one can complain and I won't get tangled up in his lines.

I got into trouble doing that as well from my Mom. Here was a lake full of fish, I was not fishing in Thorns lines and still I was getting into trouble. Mrs D wobbled over and said 'For God sake Finley! Don't swim or try catch fish so close to the rods, you scaring my Dads fish away. Go further down to those trees where you not in the way and do your swimming and fishing there. You causing chaos swimming so close to the rods'

Ahhhh, I got it! It wasn't nearly as exciting as fishing right next to Thorn, but I finally understood. It wasn't long and I had found some rats in the bushes to chase. Those rats didn't know what had hit them. They fat and lazy and I nearly had them on a few occasions.

That fishing trip was amazing for me. I had the best fun. Mrs D came swimming with me most times and we grew closer every day. She was really old, but I liked her very much. She always said it as it was and sometimes I annoyed her, but overall, we were beginning to understand each other. She taught me a lot in those early days.

We also went to Wales. Thorn wanted to introduce Mom to his Sister, Mila and her husband Thomas. As well as his Mother, Rose who had moved from Cornwall to Wales many years ago. That was another fantastic few days. We went to the beach where I swam in the sea. We all climbed rocks to do fishing. Only this time, I didn't jump in the water because even I could see it was too dangerous.

I really liked Thorns's family. They were all very kind to me. Mila and Thomas have a dog called Biscuit. A chocolate Labrador. She wasn't as old as Mrs D, but she wasn't far behind. Biscuit was lovely too. Very polite, welcomed me into her home, and showed me around the garden. Only problem really was her and Mrs D did not see eye to eye. I had my work cut out for me. Mrs D and Biscuit had fallen out a few years back and neither would tell me why.

It was that trip to Wales that got me defending Mrs D. As much as I liked Biscuit, Mrs D was now my family and I realized on that trip just how old and frail she actually was. She needed someone who had her back and I was going to be that someone. That one dog you can rely on to defend you, back you up, and generally have your corner. Beside my sense of loyalty, I owed her at least that much. She was instrumental in getting our parents together. Without her help, Mom and Thorn would probably not be together. With that in mind, I stopped Biscuit from eating Mrs D's dinner which caused friction between Biscuit and I. Mrs D appreciated the gesture very much and it allowed her to eat at her pace and in peace while I stood guard at the door.

Slowly but surely, Thorn was moving in with us. Mrs D's bed was even brought over and put in the spot she liked to sleep. We were becoming a family. During the day, we would go for long walks, go swimming and chase squirrels, and at night, Mom and Thorn would sit outside and talk. Other times, they would take us to the pub for a beer. I would cause chaos according to my Mom, because I didn't like the waiter reaching his arm out to my Mom and Thorn.

It's really unfair that I get into trouble when all I am doing is trying to keep everyone safe. It really annoys me when humans reach their hands out towards me and my family and don't get me started on that postman. That man has no manners.

Just before Thorn moved in permanently, Mom had a week from hell emotionally. She got a phone call from Esme, saying that Adam had died. Mom had been expecting it. Adam's health deteriorated daily and death was imminent. Her, and Esme had spoken often over the weeks and before her Dad slipped into a coma she had managed to have one short conversation with him. His speech was very garbled but she managed to tell him that she loved him very much and that he was always in her thoughts and prayers.

Even though she expected the call, it was still a shock when the phone rang confirming his death. She cried a lot. I didn't know what to do to console her. All I could do was to rest my head on her lap. Although she had forgiven him for doing what he did to both of us in South Africa, it had caused a big rift in their already fragile relationship. I remember she had a few whiskies that night. Thorn was away on a fishing trip that week and offered to come home but Mom said no, she just needed to morn her Dads death by herself.

Esme asked Mom if she was going to fly over for the funeral and Mom said 'No Esme. If there was a trip to be made, it should have been while he was alive and not now when he is dead. My Nana always said 'Bring me flowers while I am alive and not when I am dead' I should have brought Dad flowers while he was alive. I am not going to fly over to place flowers on his coffin. Forgive me, but I won't be attending the funeral.'

Five days later, Mom and I were sitting in the lounge and I saw Steve. I was so excited and was wagging my tail and barking. It was very confusing for me because Mom couldn't see Steve but I could. It made no sense to me. She kept asking me 'Finley who are you barking at? Who is it you can see that I can't?'

I was shouting at her 'Its Steve! Look! He is standing right here' but she didn't understand me and she couldn't see him. Steve was smiling and talking to me 'Hello Finley Boy. Calm down, you going to scare the granny out of your mother. Only you can see me Fin.'

Thinking I was talking to myself, I barked out loud 'Why? Why can I see you and not my Mom?' the last thing I expected was Steve to actually understand my barking and answer me. I nearly fell off my own paws with shock when he answered 'Finley I am dead. Before I head off on the next phase of my life, I needed to come and check on your Mom to make sure she was happy and well. To be honest Fin, I don't understand how you can see me or how I can talk to you, but this is a wonderful experience for me'

'Steve you dead? Does that mean we will never see you again?' I asked

Steve explained that although he was dead which meant we would never see him in the flesh again, he would continue to watch over us from what he called the spirit world. He said he died from a heart attack and wanted to check on Mom and I and to say goodbye. I told him all about Thorn and he said he knew about Thorn and he knew that Mom was happy and content and that was all that mattered to him. He was just so pleased that she had finally moved on from Ryan and found a genuine man, a good man, who truly loved her. Steve said he had missed us so much.

I was so sad. I had always loved Steve. I asked Steve how he was going to let Mom know and he said 'Your Mother is a very perceptive and gifted woman Fin. So when she goes to bed and is relaxed, I will do my best to get through to her.' He continued with 'Fin, look after yourself and always protect your mother. I have to go now, but I promise to visit when I can and always keep an eye on you both. I love you Fin'

'I love you too Steve' I barked and suddenly he was gone. The only person in the lounge now was Mom staring at me intently. 'Gosh Finley I wish I knew who you were talking to and who you saw, but I can feel it was a good energy. I am going to bed. Sleep tight Foo'

Following morning was chaos. Mom bounded out of bed shouting to herself 'Oh my God, Steve is dead. He can't be! No he can't be. Surely not. Please God no! That's who Finley could see last night!' she was scrambling for her phone and dialling his number and of course no one replied. She must have phoned a dozen times. I so wished she could speak dog. Instead I had to watch her emotionally unravel into a tearful heap after finally getting hold of a mutual friend Liz who said 'Danny I am so sorry. Yes Steve was found dead in his apartment. I left several messages for you on Facebook but you never replied.'

'I haven't been on Facebook for almost a year. I am so sorry. How and when did he die?' Mom asked

'We not sure exactly when he died, it could have been days ago, but the coroner says it was a cardiac arrest that killed him. I am so sorry for your loss. How did you know he was dead if you didn't go onto Facebook?' asked Liz

Mom replied with 'He told me early hours of the morning. I woke up to the weight of someone sitting on my bed. Initially I panicked and almost had my own heart attack and then I felt his presence. It was Steve. He was sitting on the side of my bed. I could feel his hand on my face and I knew. I just haven't been able to get hold of anyone to confirm'

Thorn came back from his fishing trip and he just held her and let her cry it all out. It had been a week of two deaths and a lot of tears. That day Mom and I took a walk into the woods to a place she felt safe and there she sat down and talked to Steve out loud. She felt his presence but I saw him. Strange how she saw Ryan's ghostly friend and yet couldn't see Steve.

She begged his forgiveness for not being in touch. She explained she felt too embarrassed to return his attempt at contacting her because she had gone back to Ryan. Mom poured her heart out. Steve understood everything, and he kept telling her 'Cheeky Monkey, it's all fine! I have known you almost all your life. You think I don't know what you telling me? Common now, wipe those tears. I am happy. I had a great life. I did everything I wanted to do. I leave behind no regrets at all. Also to be fair, I could have made more of an effort myself to contact you. So don't blame yourself'

She couldn't see Steve but she heard him. Mom said 'Poodle I have either lost my mind completely or I have just heard you clearly' and she started laughing. Steve she called Poodle because word has it that he used to perm his hair back in the 80's. It was a standing joke between them.

'Steve did you suffer before you passed over?' she asked

'No Cheeky, I was a gonner before I even hit the deck. It was so sudden'

'Steve, I am not going to your funeral. I just can't do it. I hope you can forgive me'

'Nothing to forgive Cheeky. Funerals are not my thing either. I did put in my will that I wanted a wake with loads of booze flowing and I want people to have fun and remember the good times and the many laughs we all shared. I hope they do as I have asked. I can't think of anything more morbid than a bunch of people sitting there balling their eyes out.'

Having spoken to Steve she felt a lot better and we made our way home. After a few weeks emotions were more stable. Both Adam and Steve's funerals had come and gone and life was returning back to normal for us.

Then one evening while they were sitting outside chatting and listening to music, Thorn got down on one knee and asked Mom to marry him 'Sir, I am so in love with you. You are the best thing that has ever happened in my life. I don't deserve someone as beautiful and loving as you, but what I feel for you is so pure. I know it's only been six months, but would you do me the honour of being my wife? I cannot see, nor want to, experience a life without you. Please say yes'

Boy was I glad Mrs D was lying outside with me or else I would have had to run inside and call her and she takes ages to walk a few steps. It would have all been over by the time she made it outside. Both of us were dead quiet. Just waiting to see how this would end.

'Thorn, I hid behind bushes, I hid behind trees, and I even hid behind my own heart. I was too scared to believe what we had was true. It was too good to be true. Yet here you are. Here we are. Yes it's only been six months, but I know that what I feel for you is real. I feel so blessed to have someone like you in my life. You are the most wonderful person I have ever met. The vortex works! Of course I will marry you. I adore you!' replied Mom

Thorn was laughing 'All I am is yours Sir. Thank you for saying yes. Now what's with the vortex?'

After they had laughed, kissed and clinked their glasses Mom explained all about the vortex and how she had placed her order for him with God and I was telling Mrs D about my vortex to Anubis which she found very interesting. Thorn gave Mom a beautiful diamond ring which I later learned was a 2 carat solitaire. We were to be a real family. Thorn was to become my Dad and Mrs D my sister. Wow! How life had changed in a few short months.

Four months later, Mom and Dad were married. Mrs D and I were over the moon with happiness. I now had two sisters, one dog and one human and I loved both Mrs D and Grubby. My greatest love beside my Mom is my Dad. He is the best Dad any dog could wish for. I love sleeping on my back in his arms while he kisses my hooter and strokes my belly. He makes me feel so safe and loved.

Our life changed overnight. Grubby moved in with her boyfriend Josh and Mom and Dad went house hunting. They wanted to find a house that had a bigger garden and more room for all of us. Mrs D and I travelled the country with them looking at houses. After all those hours and days of travelling in the boot of the car, the perfect house ended up being a stone throw from our old house. We were off the general base and Dad with the help of the military found us a wonderful big, free standing house in the Officers' Quarters which the Military were prepared to rent out privately to us.

Mrs D and I had only seen the house from the outside and it was so big. Mom and Dad walked us over one day to show us. Without Mrs D walking at a snail's pace and insisting on reading every newspaper along the way, it would have taken us ten minutes to walk there and not thirty! Well, ten minutes at the pace my Mom walks. My Dad says walking with Mom is like doing a quick march.

Not long after we saw the house Mom and Dad started packing. I hate moving and so does Mrs D. So we just tried to stay out the way as much as possible. It took them all day because it was January of the new year now and cold, wet and utterly miserable.

When we finally were allowed to be taken over both Mrs D and I were in shock at the size of the garden. I heard my Dad saying the garden was just short of an acre. Means nothing to me, all I can tell you is it is big and I love it. It has apple trees, pear trees, plum trees and blackberry bushes. They my favourite. I love plucking the blackberries off the bush and eating them. Mom and Dad just shake their head and laugh.

After we had settled in Dad said to Mom 'Sir, I think we need to get another dog. A friend for Finley. Mrs D is too old to run around and play with him. He needs a younger mate to share his balls with'

I remember saying to Mrs D 'What! Share my balls? Has Dad lost his mind completely? I will share anything at all with anyone, but I draw the line at my balls! Oh this is not good. Mrs D they thinking of getting another dog. What are we going to do? That means we have to share our beds, our garden, the sofa, Mom and Dad's bed, our hooter kisses and our belly rubs!'

'Finley, I am too tired to listen to your ramblings. Honestly! You think I like the idea of another dog that is going to knock me off my paws to get to the front door when the postman arrives? I barely manage to stand on my own four paws as it is! There is nothing we can do. Maybe this need of a friend for you will blow over.'

'Mrs D, I don't need a friend to play with. I have you. I am sorry for knocking you over. I don't mean to. It's just that postman tries to break into this house every day by putting his hand through our door and he just doesn't learn.'

Mrs D was having an off day. Her body was aching but she still took the time to try and explain 'Finley, he is not breaking in. He is delivering post. Letters. Finley you have been a good friend to me. You have brought a lot of happiness into my life and given me a reason to keep going. However, my Dad is right'

'Our Dad!' I quickly corrected her

'Our Dad' she sighed and continued 'he is right. You do need someone your own age to run around with. I cannot back you like I could have done a couple of years ago. My legs don't work like they used to. I am full of tumours and most days I feel downright sick. I hear you barking, calling me and telling me what you can see or sense. The danger close by, but I am useless to you. By the time I make my way over to back you up, the danger has moved on. I am too slow these days. You need some younger company to play and guard the house with. Hell, when I bark these days, I fall on my bum. Getting old is humiliating. I just wish you could have known me in my youth. I would have given you a run for your balls! I am living in old bones Fin. Old bones that are weak and frail.'

'Oh Mrs D, I am sorry. I never realized you feel so sick every day'

'Don't be silly Finley, I have lived a good life. My only sadness is that my Dad, our Dad, never met our Mom earlier. I would love to have had the energy to play with you and share adventures. Saying that, I am one lucky old girl to have you at my side as my brother and my dearest friend. Plus even though I am slow and read all the dog news, Mom and Dad take me for a little walk every day. They both determined to give me the best until I take my last breath. Dad lies on the floor next to my bed stroking me when I am having a bad night. It's a good life. Now cheer up and accept whatever comes with grace and before you ask me, it means accept it with good manners. I am tired and going for a lie down' with that said, Mrs D wobbled to her bed.

I didn't care much for a new friend, but if it happened, I would accept it with good manners. As you know, Mrs D is very strict on manners. For example, if Mom or Dad stand on her tail in the kitchen by mistake and don't apologise she snuffles their feet and sinks her teeth into their slippers. The minute they lean down, stroke her and say 'Sorry Mrs D' she wags her tail, moves out the way, apology accepted. But God help you if you forget to apologise.

We all settled into our new home very quickly. Mom and Dad loved the garden as much as we did. As the weather started warming up, Dad would start with the BBQ's and they were back to dancing outside, singing and enjoying every moment of their new life together. I learned so much about my Dad during that time. He is such a brave man.

Mom always says it's very sad that serving Military personal and veterans are not treated with more kindness and respect. These people put their lives on the line daily to keep our Country safe and yet they are on the list of the most neglected. My Dad was part of a specialized and highly skilled Commando unit. He and his team could and would be deployed to anywhere in the world at a moment's notice.

He was involved in maritime security operations, overseas training missions, specialist amphibious support across the defence and so much more. He did a several tours in Afghanistan, Iraq, Ireland and many other Countries. I heard him telling Mom he was a Jungle Warfare Instructor, an Artic Survivor Instructor, a Royal Marines Training Instructor and he even received a medal from the Queen of England. I can't remember all the things he has done but it was so interesting to just lie there and listen to his stories. A lot of it to be honest, I didn't fully understand, but I knew I was so proud of him.

Some things he would not discuss with Mom. There is the chunk of his life which he says is classified. 'Is there no amount of wine or whisky that will loosen your tongue Thorn?'

Mom would ask while laughing and his reply was always the same 'No Sir. It's classified. That is just the way it is'

My Mom lived through a war in what was called Rhodesia and is today known as Zimbabwe. The war lasted for fifteen years and was known as The Zimbabwe War of Liberation. She was eleven years old when it ended. Gosh between my Mom and my Dad they have both experienced quite a lot and shared many stories that kept Mrs D and I glued to their feet.

I love my Dad. Nothing in the world upsets him. He never gets angry. I have never heard him raise his voice. He will sit on the floor if I am lying on the sofa and being stretched out on my back, I take up all the space. He is the most incredible man ever and I thank Anubis every day for bringing him into our lives.

Three months after we had moved in and many evening BBQ's and military chats later, Mom came out holding her phone 'Thorn look at this dog. He is beautiful. These people are looking for a new home for him and they only want £75. Look I know it's a good price but do they even realise the dangers out there? To advertise a dog like this for £75 is so dangerous. He could fall into the wrong hands too easily. What do you think?'

'He is beautiful. Have you sent them a message?' Dad asked

'Yes I have and she has replied saying that there are several people coming to view him and she will let me know if he is still available in a few days' time. God I pray he finds a good home. Look Fin and Mrs D, what do you guys think?'

Mrs D and I glanced at the screen. For my Moms sake, I wagged my tail, but deep down, if I am honest, I thought he was too pretty. I wasn't keen for this dog to come live with us. Just the thought of my Dad fussing over another dog depressed me. Mrs D said 'Finley, you need to calm down. You can't tell anything by a photo. You heard Mom, it's going to take a few days. There are loads of people going to look at him, one of them will probably take him.'

No. My gut was telling me he was destined to end up with us and I couldn't shake the feeling off. I was proved right in my feelings. One week later, and after many messages sent from my Mom, the lady phoned and said no one had wanted him. Would Mom like her to drive him over so she could meet him?

Both Mom and Dad were very excited. Mom told the lady 'please bring his bedding, toys and food bowls if you can. If not, don't worry we have enough of everything. I can't wait to meet him'

On Friday the 13th March, Stryder arrived. Well, his name then was Bingo, but Mom changed it the following day to Stryder. Mrs D and I were outside when the car pulled up. Mom had asked the woman to please let Stryder out, so the three of us could meet on neutral ground. She wanted to see how we all got along.

I could have sabotaged that day, but there was something very vulnerable about Stryder. There was a sadness. A loneliness that I had seen all too often. This dog needed and deserved a home like ours. A home filled with love and laughter. Where a dog is part of the family as my Mom and Dad always say. We all instantly liked him. Stryder had been brought up by an Eastern European family and his English was very rusty.

Within minutes of Stryder's arrival and with the car not even unpacked yet, Mom reached into her pocket and gave the lady £75. Bingo had a new home, a new brother and sister, a new Mom and Dad, a new name the following day, and a whole new life ahead of him.

Mom and Dad gushed over his looks. My Dad said he is the only 'Beautiful' boy in the world. I was handsome, good looking, and Stryder was beautiful. Even though the word beautiful was usually reserved for girls, I have to agree, he was very pretty. I heard Mom and Dad telling everyone that Stryder is a traditional Scotch Collie.

'I believe the breed was originally from Scotland several centuries ago. His ancestors are believed to include Celtic Dogs and Viking Herding Spitzers' Mom told Nan and went on to say 'Mom, wait until you meet him. He is like a painting. Pure perfection. His markings. His eyes! He looks like he has black eyeliner on and his one eye has a blue star in it. He is truly the most magnificent looking boy. He is very nervous though and taking a little bit of strain which is natural'

It's true. Initially Stryder found it difficult to settle in. Mrs D and I tried to talk to him and although he understood a lot of what we were saying, he was feeling betrayed. That first night with Stryder and before Mom changed his name, I said to him 'Bingo, welcome to our home. I know you must be scared but please don't be. I am here if you want to talk. Mrs D is very old, but very wise and she is an excellent listener. So if you need either of us, just let us know'

Stryder just ignored me. Mom walked past him to sort his bed out and he snuffled her feet and bit her toes through her slippers. Mom got a big fright 'Bingo! That is not very nice. I am trying to sort your bed out so you more comfortable. Biting me is not good.'

'Bingo, don't bite my Mom and Dad please. They only trying to help you' I told him.

'Leave me alone' was his reply.

Mrs D called me into the passage way 'Finley, he is scared. Just leave him to settle in his own time. It's all new for him and he doesn't have a clue where his family have gone and doesn't understand why he has been left with total strangers. He is going to need time to adjust. It must be awful thinking you going out for a drive in the car and suddenly you find yourself being dumped on people who don't speak your language.'

She was right. I would stay out of his way until he made an effort to come forward. I was sure my Mom and Dad could defend their own toes. That evening I heard them talking about Stryder and Mom said that Stryder's last family had caged him for 11 hours a day. All he had known from being a puppy, was life in a cage.

Mom and Dad were very upset and said that if you cannot make a dog part of your family, then you should not have one. It is beyond cruel to cage a dog for hours on end. My Mom and Dad were very upset that Stryder had lived like this for so long.

'What mental and emotional damage has been done?' Mom asked my Dad

'It is shameful. Truly sad that some people lack so much soul. They simply cannot understand a dog or any animals for that matter.' my Dad replied.

He went on to tell Mom about a dog he knew in Afghanistan. This family had an Asian Shepherd that was chained up 24/7. The owners said it made the dog vicious and that it was protecting their home. My Dad could see the dog was slowly going mad and spent a long time trying to explain to the man that when a dog is made a part of the family, they will defend you with their life. By keeping it chained to a runner, it can only protect a meter either side of the runner. Just imagine if you could build a trust with your dog that was so deep and so strong that it would allow him to protect your whole property including your children.

My Dad said the whole situation had to be handled very delicately because it was not their culture to allow a dog to be a part of the inner circle. After many hours and visits, the man said he would give it a try. My Dad left Afghanistan and on his next tour of duty, he went to check on the dog and found it running loose with the children. The owner thanked my Dad for talking and explaining everything to him. He also said the dog loved the children and no one could come near them.

The dog slept in the house and was now the most important family member. He was fed well and given a blanket on the floor to sleep on because he was the protector of not only the farm but the family. The man told my Dad that the dog had saved his life twice since the last time they had seen each other.

Then one day my Dad noticed that Stryder's canines had been filed down. He phoned the vet who was horrified and said they refuse to do that at their surgery. He said it is common in Europe for herding dogs to have their teeth filed so they don't injure the sheep. In England however, it was frowned upon and considered cruel to many veterinary practices. It looked like Stryder had not had the best life and he still wasn't talking.

Mom was moaning to my Dad 'Why do so many people find it perfectly acceptable to file a dogs teeth down and cage an animal in the morning before leaving for work. Have they ever stopped to think what that must be like for the dog? How would they feel, if every day for the rest of their lives, their husband, wife, girlfriend, boyfriend, partner, put them into the pantry and locked the door for 11 hours a day? You have limited, to no movement. If you need a wee or a poo you either hold onto it or soil your pantry or cage.

Then when the person who holds the key to your cage or pantry comes home, they furious with you because you couldn't hold onto your bladder or your bowels and now they have to clean up after you. So you have not only been alone and locked up all day, you now being shouted at and probably getting a hiding because they have just walked in from work and are tired, irritable and probably at their wits end from a really shitty day. Now they have to clean up after you. Do they even for one minute think how sore your body is from lying in the same position for all those hours? How your joints ache?

Then they let you out after screaming at you and cleaning you and the mess up, and you have only a short time to stretch your legs, your back, enjoy a little bit of freedom, before being put back in the cage for the night because a human has decided that you like it in your cage. It's your 'safe' place. How deluded humans are.

What is the purpose of having a dog if that is how you treat it? Those people should be ashamed of themselves.'

Mom and Dad are very against caging and the results were clear to see in Stryder. He took ages to understand that he was free and that he could go outside when he felt like it. He was free to run off a lead. He was free to sleep on the sofa or climb on the bed in the mornings for hooter kisses and belly rubs. It took him ages to understand that he was free because he was loved and trusted.

In this new home, no one would ever lock him up. He was now a part of a family. He was treated with nothing but love and respect and in the end that is what won Stryder over. Love was Stryder's healer. Not Mrs D. Not me. Only unconditional love. That love had healed not only Mom, but my Dad, Mrs D, myself and now Stryder.

After almost three months, Stryder was one of us. As I got to know Stryder, I liked him more and more. We grew closer by the day. There was something strangely familiar about him. I felt like I had met him before. Then I decided that I was really starting to sound too much like my Mom. But Stryder really was familiar.

One day after going through the woods for a long walk we got home and were exhausted. Stryder and I lay in the lounge on the carpet and I asked him how he was enjoying his new home and I asked him if he missed his other family and to share his life with me.

'Finley, when I used to be locked in that cage, I used to dream of being a part of a family like this. My dreams are what kept me going. I would lie there for eleven hours a day seeing myself running free. Being able to wee and poo when I needed to and not holding onto it for hours.

I would see a loving family who loved me and I loved them. I dreamt about this life. It was a tough life for me Fin. I got taken away from my Mother very young. I cried so much when I got picked up and chucked in a cage and onto the back of a van. I didn't know where I would end up. I cried many a night for my Mother. She was a breeding bitch and had the most awful life.

Then one day after days of travelling I woke up and these people were there to take me to my new home. I didn't know at the time what type of life I would have. In their own way, I guess they liked me, but they never loved me. I was a toy for their children to play with. From the day I arrived I was caged. First for toilet training, and then because it was easier for them.

As the children grew they never realized it but they used to hurt me. So I would snap at them. I never meant to hurt them but they would pull me by my ears, or sit on me and I couldn't breathe. So I would bite out in pain. That is when my parents decided to file my teeth down.

I would be in that cage all day and then when they did come home, they wanted to get their chores sorted out before letting me out the cage. Every day I was in agony from holding my wee and poo. Also my back ached terribly. I couldn't get out soon enough and often the minute they opened the cage, the kids would jump on me and many times I just couldn't hold my bladder and I would get a terrible hiding.

To be honest I never realized how much it had affected me. I became aggressive and very antisocial. I heard them talking about giving me away. I didn't care at that stage. My emotional state was so low, they could have put me on the street and I would have been a lot happier with life scrounging for food than being locked up and treated like I was.

So many people came to see me and I didn't like any of them. So I showed my aggressive side and they all disappeared. The day we arrived here I knew you were all good people. I was just so tired and fed up. I was scared but I knew one thing, I did not want to go home with my old family. When I came into your house, I couldn't believe my eyes, no cage in sight. I saw all the dog beds and it was really difficult to imagine sleeping on a bed and not in a cage.

Also your Mom changed my name and I love my name Stryder. It was a new name for a new life.

I love my new Mom and Dad so much and I love you and Mrs D. You have all been so patient, kind, and given me the love I needed to heal. I can only hope that somehow my birth Mother knows that I am finally happy and I am with a family that I love with all my heart.'

I had lain there listening and watching Stryder as the emotions were running through him. Again, I felt this sense of familiarity. Why? I told Stryder I would be back and that I just needed to go for a wee. I didn't need a wee, I just needed some time out to think. It was while standing picking a few blackberries from the hedge that it hit me.

Could it be? Was it even possible? I ran at full speed back into the house.

'Stryder? Stryder?' I was barking for him

'For god sake Finley, I am not well today, keep the noise down will you' moaned Mrs D

'Mrs D, you gonna want to hear this story. Get up and come lie in the lounge'

Mrs D struggled to get up but managed to wobble through to the lounge and lay down on the carpet.

'What's up Fin? I heard you calling me but I was upstairs with Dad getting hooter kisses'

'Stryder, this is going to sound crazy, but is your mother's name Millie?' I asked

'Yes! How did you know?' replied Stryder in absolute shock.

'Blue Star!' is all I said

Stryder was staring at me like he had seen a ghost. Mrs D was watching and waiting with me for the answer. She knew my whole life story and she knew all about 'Blue Star' and how I was called Wolf Eyes.

'Well?' I pushed Stryder

Stryder was transfixed. Then he gasped as the penny dropped 'Finley Wolf Eyes! Son of Bikkie'

'Yes! Yes! Yes!' I was barking with joy.

After six years Anubis had woven a plan and brought Blue Star right into our home.

What an incredible life journey we have all had. Stryder wanted to know all about my life and how I had ended up with my Mom and Dad. What experiences I have lived and the places I had visited. He wanted to know everything from the day the Van pulled out of the puppy farm with all of us in cages heading for a life unknown.

It was going to be a long night.

THE END

Printed in Great Britain
by Amazon